Priceless Excel Tips at Your Fingertips

By

Sudhir Diddee

Copyright and Disclaimer

Send comments to book@vyanjan.com

ISBN-13: 978-1482047134

ISBN-10: 1482047136

Library of Congress Control Number: 2013901764

To Sujaya and Sailesh

Acknowledgements

There is an interesting folklore about Excel that when the product was conceived some twenty-two years ago, the team set a vision to create the best spreadsheet program ever created. Boy, did they succeed! This book represents the effort of thousands of engineers and product managers of the Excel team who have given us one of my favorite programs. These extremely talented and passionate people, who have thought long and hard on various aspects of our everyday analytic, charting and productivity needs, make it easier for all of us. This book stands on the shoulders of those giants.

I have been fortunate to work in a great company and have been influenced by Microsoft Co-founder Bill Gates and Microsoft CEO Steve Ballmer, who have instilled a solid, data-driven culture. It is no secret that Microsoft business reviews often border on the edge of being "math camps" if your numbers don't add up. This high expectation of data analysis has shaped the DNA of Microsoft. Excel has to pass Microsoft's own benchmarks first, which means each subsequent version pushes the boundaries of excellence ever further.

I would like to thank my editors Leigh-Anne, Christine Willmsen and my designer Kris Hamper. There are the wonderful executives, smart managers and colleagues, too many to list here, with whom I am fortunate to work and learn from every day, and who make my company truly the best place to work.

Finally, I need to thank my wife Seema for her unwavering support (who let me write this book as I approached the goal we set for my first book), and my kids Abhinav and Ananya for being extremely patient as I worked long weekends, nights and holidays. The amount of time the book took to write was captured by a simple sentiment from my daughter, who said, "Daddy only likes to sit at the computer on Saturdays. Can you give up the addiction to the computer?"

I hope the long hours really add value to some readers' lives.

Table of Contents

Intended Audience

This book is intended for the average office worker who may be curious about or a little intimidated by Excel. It is for someone who wants or needs to get better at Excel. If you are a financial analyst or spend more than two hours a day in Excel, you would probably know more than half the tips in this book. However, I took care to include tips which even some of my finance colleagues admitted were unknown to them.

In my experience, most modern-day office workers are familiar with some features of commonly used software. However, either due to lack of time or being just plain afraid to try new things we stop pushing ourselves. With software, the sky is the limit and literally no one can call himself or herself an expert as the boundaries are being pushed all the time at a pace that is impossible to keep up with.

One of the challenges in learning is to implement the learning at work. I am an avid reader, and I find translating the skills learned in books to my actual work life takes a lot of conscious effort and is extremely hard. I tried to write this book and categorize it in a format in which users can self-select any topic and dive straight into it or go chapter by chapter from beginning to end.

How to use this book

Excel is a spreadsheet program for organizing and manipulating data. With some bit of mastery over Excel, not only will you be able to crunch numbers faster but also you will be able to derive better insights from data.

The skills are in an increasing order of difficulty; intermediate users can start from the fourth or fifth tip of a section and go to the end. Advanced users should still find about 25-30 new tips. I deliberately stayed away from statistics and advanced quantitative techniques as there are many excellent books on the topic and it does not address my audience.

As with everything in life, changing old habits is hard. The same is true for benefiting from the tips in this book. Various research scholars on human behavior have suggested that it takes 21 days to form a habit. I think that is a good benchmark. The best way to use this book is to take any one section at a time and practice the tips until they become second nature.

You should review **The Windows Graphical User Interface** and **The Excel Interface** in the Appendix to familiarize yourself with the elements of a program window, to make the most of these tips. Take a printout of the Cheat Sheet at the end of the book and pin it next to your computer at work and home. Every time you want to save time using one of the tips, check yourself if you fall back to doing it the old way. Soon you will be addicted to the new method.

Finally, the best way to learn is to teach others and push yourself to take on harder problems. There is no substitute for practice. Remember to be curious. There is a community of passionate users out there willing to teach and learn. I learned these over the years through friends, colleagues, websites and sheer curiosity. If you come across a valuable tip, please feel free to e-mail me at: book@vyanjan.com

I hope you have as much fun using this book as I had writing it.

This is a very different kind of book. A user can either go by section or go by the level of difficulty. If you think you are an intermediate user then you can probably just read Tips 7 through 10 of each section. If you consider yourself to be an advanced reader, you might just review tips 9 and 10 of each section, and the section on Advanced Tips. Even if you apply 25 tips to your day-to-day life you will notice a quantum improvement in Excel output and your ability to derive insights from data.

	B	C	D	E	F	G	H	I	J	K	L
1	Difficulty Level	○	○	◔	◔	◑	◑	◕	◕	●	●
2	Section	Tip 1	Tip 2	Tip 3	Tip 4	Tip 5	Tip 6	Tip 7	Tip 8	Tip 9	Tip 10
3	Basic	Templates	Quick Scroll	Quick Zoom	Status bar	Format numbers in a cell	Formatting large numbers	Create a formula	AutoSave	Tile Excel workbooks	Create new Worksheet
4	Navigation	Jump to last Row/Column	Auto adjust Column Width	Jump to any spreadsheet	Insert Current Time/ Date Quickly	Autofill	Custom Autofill	Fill Weekdays	Quick Close	Freeze Panes	Moving sheets
5	Data Management/ Validation	Hide / Unhide sheet	Faster data entry	Sorting	Sorting by Color	Remove duplicates	Conditional formatting	Transpose	Filter	Create a drop down list	Add a dialog on data entry
6	Formulas	View all Formulae at Once	Absolute Reference	Remove formulas Keep Values	Remove numbers keep formulas	Date Calculations	Hide formula error	Formula range and named formulas	Auto Multiply	Protect formula	Auditing
7	Presentation and Packaging	Colored Tabs	Cell Styles	Printing	Margins	Header and Footer	Image as background	Insert Picture	Remove Gridlines	Group/ Ungroup	Subtotal
8	Charting	Quick Chart	Chart Types	Legend, Axes, titles	Secondary Axis	Reusable Chart Template	Excel Sparklines	Box and Whisker chart	Waterfall chart	Bubble Chart	Change Marker Symbol
9	Text Management	Wrap Text	New line data text entry	Merge and Center	Alignment	Insert Comment	Show all comments	Printing Comments of a cell	Bullets in Excel	Change Case	Concatenate
10	Pivot Table	Pivot Table	Show Values as	Count, Sum, Average	Format	Slicers	Drill down on Pivot Table	Pivot chart	Calculated Field	Calculated Item	Add Rank to a PivotTable
11	More Pivot Table and Advanced Tricks	Copy Cell Contents	Move selection	Quick Format shortcuts	Change Gridline color	Change position of Quick Access Toolbar	Change shape of a comment	Create customized Tab	Watch Window	Advanced Filter	Sensitivity Analysis
12	More Pivot Table and Advanced Tricks	Goal Seek	Scenario Manager	vlookup	Text to Columns	Views	Custom Ordering of Pivot Tables	Frequency distribution of a Pivot Table	Hide Cell content	Excel Camera Tool	

Figure 1

The 4 a.m. Phone Call

"Hello!" I said as I struggled with the phone while picking it up.

"Sudhir - I need a book on Excel!" the voice on the other side of the phone said. I was groggy as I picked up the phone. Rubbing my eyes I looked at the time, 4:05 am. Who on earth would have the audacity to call me at such an ungodly hour? Since I am a night owl, I had slept only a few hours by now and my family knows when to reach me.

Only two sorts of people can call you at such an odd hour – either drunks or old, old friends. And in my case it was my buddy Sonal. I had sent him the link earlier in the day of my first book, on Windows 7 and Office 2010, and he read the e-mail at the end of workday, 5:30 p.m. in India, and he just called me up. He had an order to place and he came straight to the point. Sonal is a world traveler and runs a pretty big organization; however, he has often confided in me that he could do better on Excel, if only he had time. We had actually spent time here and there on Excel via phone, but it was not enough.

When I mentioned to my friends and old colleagues that I had written my first book, almost everyone thought it must be on Excel, given my fascination with data and numbers. Instead, it was on Microsoft Outlook, another passion of mine. As I spoke to friends in the technology sector, many developers and program managers, to my surprise, mentioned they could definitely use help on Excel. I was quite surprised, but quickly understood why. These technically brilliant people had no time, and often the books available are intimidating, hence they never got started. Many of them have written software that is invariably touching your life today. But like you, they are busy. They know they are missing out on something, and they needed a solution.

This book is designed for beginners to intermediate users, and hopefully even advanced users will find a few tips which are new to them. I wanted to write the book in a format that cuts to the chase and gets users up and running. The idea is that a user who spends three to six hours with this book should learn a lot of new tricks and can begin reaping productivity gains right away.

Also these are *my favorite tips,* but they are in no particular order. Since Excel is so exhaustive no single book or author could ever possibly capture all these features in one book. These tips are tested on Office 2010 and I intend to update it for Windows 8 and Office 2013 in due course. However, many features should work in most versions of Excel. I recommend you try it, and if these don't work for you, consider migrating to a newer version of Microsoft Office.

Excel Basics

Microsoft Excel is the business world's preferred number-crunching program. It can be used to perform tasks from basic math calculations to advanced scientific spreadsheets, with an amazing array of functions and formulas built in to help you. With the built-in charting tools and data pivot capabilities, you have at your fingertips one of the best software programs ever built.

1. Templates

Let us begin with the uses of Excel. One of the best-kept secrets of Excel is that, while it is the de facto program for crunching numbers, it is also an excellent resource for managing text. In fact, I would not be surprised if more people use Excel for text management than for number crunching. Think of text management as maintaining lists, calendars, recipes, fitness logs, household budgets, wedding planning, etc.

While you might have various ideas or you might be using your own repository of Excel best practice templates, I would encourage you to go to Office Online and look through a whole repository of pre-built templates, both free and paid, that you may use to suit your needs. Go to http://office.microsoft.com and select **Excel** in the drop down box.

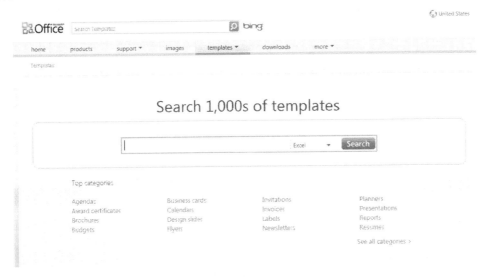

Figure 2

Here you will find all sorts of templates that you may filter by product version.

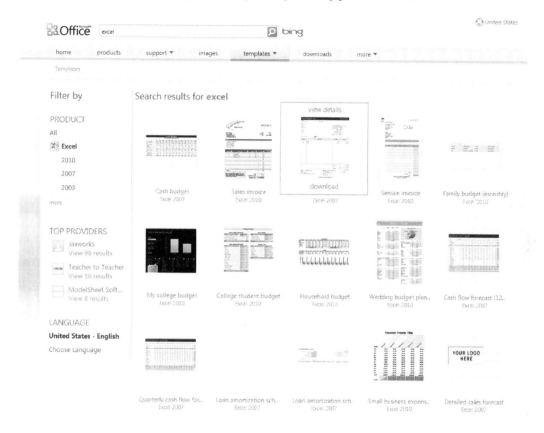

Figure 3

Here is a sample from the household budget. Just click on download, accept terms of service and save it to your templates.

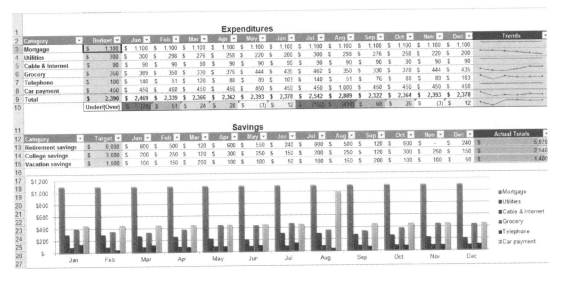

Figure 4

Now all you have to do is populate it with your data and you are good to go. If you are a relatively inexperienced user or an occasional user then this is the way to get a head start with professional-looking spreadsheets. Even if you are an experienced user, this is the way to go. You will be surprised by how many people have no clue such a fantastic resource exists and hence I put this tip right in the beginning.

2. Quick Scroll

This tip works if you are using a mouse that has a scroll wheel.

To quickly scroll through the various tabs in Excel on the excel ribbon, just move the cursor anywhere on the ribbon and move the mouse scroll wheel forward or backward to scroll through the tabs. The tab is a set of related commands grouped together.

For example, moving the scroll wheel moves the cursor from Home to Insert, Page Layout, Formulas etc.

Figure 5

Note: see the appendix to acquaint yourself with the parts of an Excel 2010 spreadsheet

3. Quick Zoom

This is again one of those quick tips that is easy to remember and makes you very productive right from the start.

Click on the active spreadsheet and click CTRL+ MOUSE SCROLLWHEEL backward or forward to Zoom out or Zoom in. Here is a little secret, it works in Microsoft Word and Microsoft PowerPoint as well.

4. Status Bar

Before we get into the detailed tips, I want to share this tip. Most experienced users of Excel are familiar with this, but those who use it infrequently will start getting much more productive straight away.

Say you have a list of salespersons and their commissions in the month of January.

	A	B	C	D	E
1	Commission Earned in the month of January				
2	Salesperson	Commision($)			
3	Stanley	$ 566			
4	Martin	$ 626			
5	Emma	$ 359			
6	John	$ 730			
7	George	$ 605			
8	Alan	$ 393			
9	Cindy	$ 279			
10	Richard	$ 525			
11	Kaylee	$ 290			
12	Caroline	$ 456			
13	Jean	$ 727			
14	Shirley	$ 344			
15	Peter	$ 794			
16	April	$ 724			
17					

Figure 6

I just have 14 names here, but say you have 40 or 50 rows of data, and you want to know the average, total commission paid, number of cells with data, etc.

Just "paint" or select the cells, and Excel automatically shows the quick result at the bottom right of the screen. We can see the average is $530, the count of cells with values is 14, and sum is $7,418.

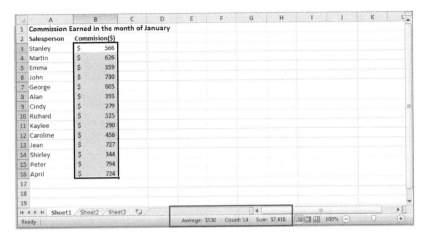

Figure 7

If you right click on the status bar you can customize it for your own needs by checking and unchecking the options you want.

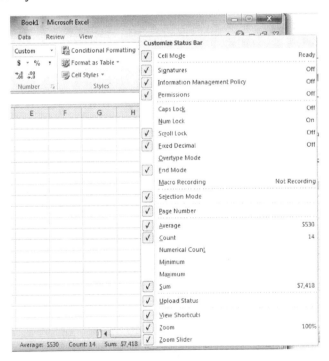

Figure 8

5. Format Numbers in a Cell

To quickly format the numbers in a cell, select the cell and hit **CTRL+1**:

▲	A	B	C	D	E
1	Item	Price	Quanity	Total	
2	Paint	$ 22.95	2	$ 45.90	
3	Paint Rolle	$ 6.95	4	$ 27.80	
4	Masking ta	$ 4.95	5	$ 24.75	
5	Sandpaper	$ 0.95	10	$ 9.50	
6	Caulking	$ 3.95	2	$ 7.90	
7	Mixing Bru	$ 5.95	1	$ 5.95	
8	Wire Brush	$ 1.95	2	$ 3.90	
9					

Figure 9

You will see the formatting window where you can select the option that applies to the cell.

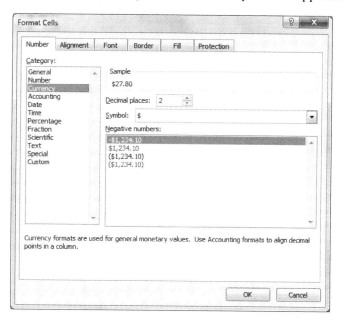

Figure 10

Here are some useful tips to format a cell quickly:

- CTRL+SHIFT+~ - Applies the General number format.
- CTRL+SHIFT+$ - Applies the Currency format with two decimal places.
- CTRL+SHIFT+% - Applies the Percentage format with no decimal places.

6. Formatting large numbers

People who need to work with big numbers often need a format that is easily consumable. Let us say you are reporting traffic and page views to a top website, or you need to report the revenue of your business unit, which is in the millions. Many times the seven-digit numbers make it hard to follow the trend or glean useful insights, but one of the ways is to format the cells in millions or thousands.

Here is an example:

Product Unit	Sales	Profit
Ski's	$13,131,434	$ 399,838
Bicycles	$18,313,013	$ 193,236
ATV	$21,817,958	$ 477,500
Boats	$10,331,877	$ 724,421
Kayaks	$15,598,718	$ 604,764
Snowboards	$24,378,872	$ 310,866

Figure 11

However, to make it more readable you can format the Sales in millions and Profit in thousands. To do this here are the steps:

Step 1 – Select the cells for the Sales column
Step 2- Go to Format, Custom and enter #,, i.e. the symbol # followed by two commas. If you want to show one decimal you can show $#,,.0
Step 3 – Label the column Sales as "Sales ($ millions)"
Step 4 – Select the cells for the Profit column
Step 5 – Go to Format, Custom and enter $#,.0 to format the numbers in thousands.
Step 6 – Label the column Profit as "Profit ($ thousands)"

	A	B	C	D
1	Product Unit	Sales ($ Millions)	Profit ($ '000)	
2	Ski's	$13.13	$399.8	
3	Bicycles	$18.31	$193.2	
4	ATV	$21.82	$477.5	
5	Boats	$10.33	$724.4	
6	Kayaks	$15.60	$604.8	
7	Snowboards	$24.38	$310.9	
8				

Figure 12

7. Creating a Formula

This is a well-known trick for anyone who really knows Microsoft Excel. And for the rest of us, it is immensely helpful. I dedicate this tip to a good friend who is nothing short of a genius in his field of computer science. I call him Raja (which stands for king in India) of coding. My friend can literally dissect any operating system or any piece of software in a matter of hours. But, one day I saw him struggling with something and asked why was he hesitant in using Microsoft Excel for what he was trying to accomplish. He told me point blank (as only friends can) that he did not know Microsoft Excel well enough, since he didn't use it in his day-to-day work. This was probably the only time I felt we were peers in terms of level of intelligence.

For all the folks who have never written a formula in Microsoft Excel, it is easier than you think, and more helpful than you can imagine. Here is how it works:

Let us say you have three labeled columns: one is "item," the second is "unit price," and the third is "quantity." You want to calculate the total for each row. Looking at the figure below, go to the Total column for Paint, and find cell D2. This refers to the intersection of Column D, Row 2. Click on that empty cell and simply type in **B2 * C2** preceded by an "=" sign, and you're done. The "="sign indicates to Excel that whatever follows is a formula. You have just told Excel to multiply (the asterisk means "multiply") what it finds in cell B2 and in cell C2, and to give you the answer in Column D2.

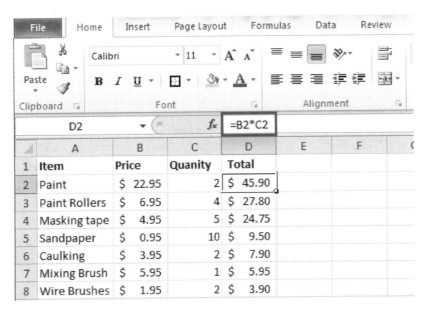

Figure 13

The standard mathematical operators will apply, and Microsoft Excel uses the symbol "*" for multiplication, "/" for division, "+" for addition, and "–"for subtraction. A formula must always start with the equal sign, as in: =B2*C2.

These formulas in Excel are so powerful that many financial and business professionals make their living crunching Excel spreadsheets filled with very complex multi-level formulae. But even knowing only the most basic types of formulas will keep your budget or inventory spreadsheets singing. And when you later have to update one part of the spreadsheet, everything downstream of that change will automatically update. For instance, if cell B2 in our example was doubled, the answer in D2 would change appropriately.

You will find Microsoft Excel functions in the following categories:

Database functions
Date and time functions
Engineering functions
Financial functions
Information functions
Logical functions
Lookup and reference functions
Math and trigonometry functions
Statistical functions
Text functions

8. Auto Save

A friend of mine called me one day at 8 p.m.

"Sudhir, I am at work and there was a power surge in my building and my PC rebooted. I have lost four hours of my work in Excel and I am hysterical. No, I am **beyond** hysterical."

I said, "I am sure you have Auto Save turned on."

"What is THAT?" she said.

I knew we had a problem. A BIG problem.

The story above did not have a happy ending but we ensured that we fixed the Auto Save setting in her Excel. If you want to avoid the same fate, here are the steps.

Step 1 – Go to File, Info, Options

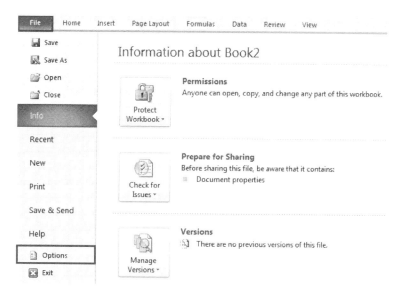

Figure 14

Step 2 – Go to the **Save section**, and check the box "**Save AutoRecover information every** X minutes" (I suggest every two minutes), give it a custom setting and click **OK.**

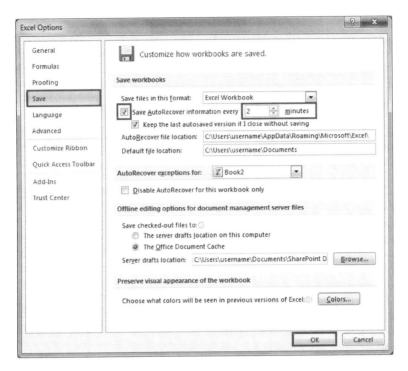

Figure 15

9. Tile two Excel workbooks side by side, or Excel Snap

Often you are working on two workbooks simultaneously and you may want to refer to one or the other, back and forth. One solution is to use **ALT+Tab** to toggle between each open program. Or the better way might be to have the workbooks tile next to each other, or snap side-by-side in the same screen.

To do this, here are the steps:

Step 1 – Open the two workbooks
Step 2 – Go to either workbook and navigate to **File, View, Arrange All**

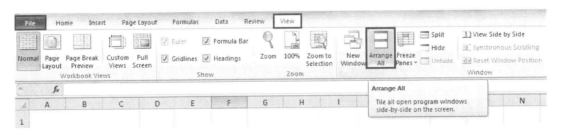

Figure 16

Step 3 – Choose any of the options Tiled, Horizontal, Vertical, etc.

Figure 17

The output will look like this. As you click on any workbook, that becomes active and the Excel ribbon works for that sheet. Some people like to work in Tiled mode, others prefer Horizontal.

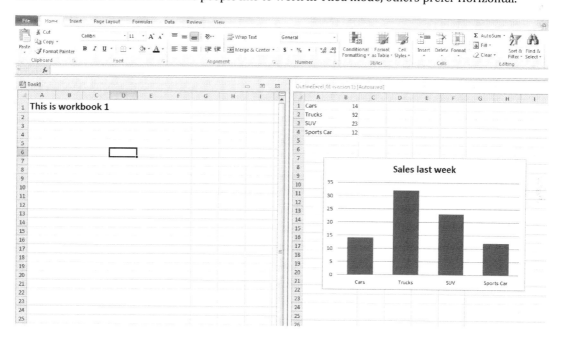

Figure 18

10.   Create a new worksheet / copy a worksheet

Since one of the goals of this book is to also add productivity to your day-to-day tasks you can insert a new Microsoft Excel worksheet by pressing **SHIFT+F11**.

To select an entire sheet, click on the corner between Column A and Row 1 as shown below in red.

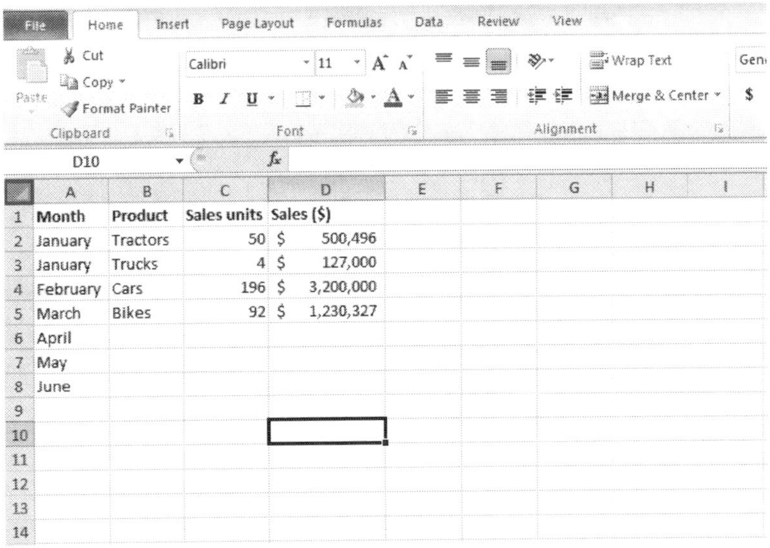

Figure 19

To copy the entire sheet selection and paste it onto a new tab or new workbook, select the data you want to move, then use **CTRL+ C** to copy your existing data and **CTRL+ V** to paste it into the new sheet.

Here is a little-known Power Trick: If you want to copy a set of cells, just select the cells and hit CTRL+C to copy them and go to the new destination cell and just hit **ENTER**. No need to hit CTRL+V.

Navigation

11. Jump to Last Row/ Column in Table with Double-Click

Select any cell in the table and double-click on the cell-border in the direction you want to go:

	A	B	C
1	Item	Price	Quanity
2	Paint	$ 22.95	2
3	Paint Rollers	$ 6.95	4
4	Masking tape	$ 4.95	5
5	Sandpaper	$ 0.95	10
6	Caulking	$ 3.95	2
7	Mixing Brush	$ 5.95	1
8	Wire Brushes	$ 1.95	2

Figure 20

Double-click on the A2 bottom border if you want to go to the last populated cell in the column or the A2 right border, for the row:

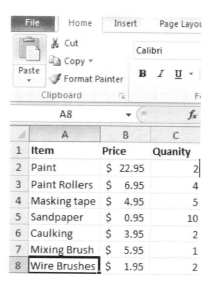

Figure 21

15

Fast Scroll

To quickly go to the last populated cell of a row or column, select a cell and hit **CTRL + Down Arrow**, or **CTRL+→**, and so on.

To quickly switch to the next worksheet, press Ctrl+PgDn

To quickly switch to the previous worksheet, press Ctrl+PgUp

12. Automatically Adjust Column Width

Adjust column widths to the correct width for each, all at one time, by selecting multiple columns and double-clicking on the separators between two of the columns' letters at the top. This trick also works if you want to adjust row heights as well (use the separators between the rows' numbers).

To adjust the width of several columns at once, select multiple columns and adjust the width on one of them by dragging the column separator – the rest will snap to that same width.

	A	B	C	D	E
1	Item	Price	Quanity	Total	
2	Paint	$ 22.95	2	$ 45.90	
3	Paint Rolle	$ 6.95	4	$ 27.80	
4	Masking ta	$ 4.95	5	$ 24.75	
5	Sandpaper	$ 0.95	10	$ 9.50	
6	Caulking	$ 3.95	2	$ 7.90	
7	Mixing Bru	$ 5.95	1	$ 5.95	
8	Wire Brush	$ 1.95	2	$ 3.90	

Figure 22

13. Jump to Any Spreadsheet

Right-click on the worksheet navigation arrows (bottom left, in yellow) and it will produce a list of all of your active tabs in your workbook. You can click on the list to go straight to that worksheet. This is very handy for workbooks with a lot of worksheets and is much faster than scrolling.

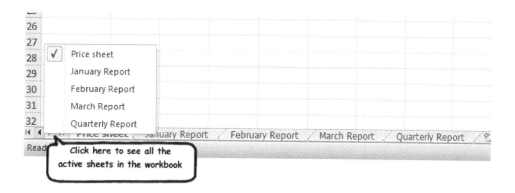

Figure 23

Right-clicking on the status bar gives you the count, sum and average of your selection. The currently highlighted range is illustrated below:

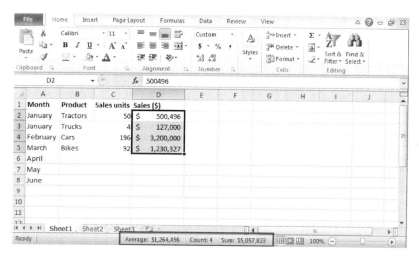

Figure 24

14.   Insert Current Time/ Date Quickly

To quickly insert the Date or Time in an Excel spreadsheet:

Current date: Press **CTRL+SEMICOLON**
Current time: Press **CTRL+SHIFT+ SEMICOLON**
Current date and time: Press **CTRL+ SEMICOLON** then **SPACE + CTRL+SHIFT+ SEMICOLON**

15.   Auto Fill

Auto Fill is priceless; it will make your life so much easier. In Auto Fill, you drag the fill handle next to a number to easily create a number series. To find the fill handle, select a populated cell, then click and drag the bottom right corner.

By dragging the fill handle of a cell, you can copy the contents of that cell, including formulas, to other cells in the same row or column.

If the cell contains a number, date, or time period that Microsoft Excel can project in a series, the values are incremented instead of copied. This saves you time in, say, numbering your rows: if you enter the number 1 in a cell and drag it down, it will copy the number 1 into the next several cells. If you enter a 1, then a 2, and select both cells, *then* drag it down, you now have 3, 4, 5, and 6 happily following.

Try it with January/February or Quarter 1/Quarter 2. You can also create a custom fill series for frequently used text entries, such as your company's sales regions.

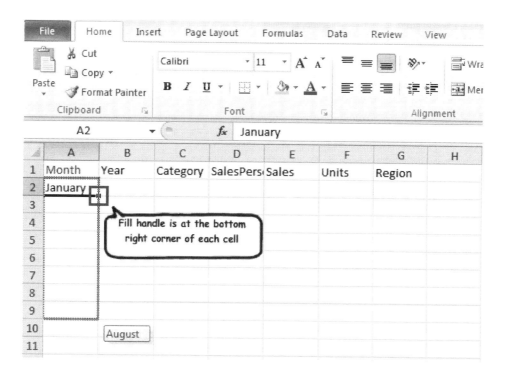

Figure 25

Automatically fill data

You can double-click the fill handle of a selected cell to fill the contents of the cell down a column for the same number of rows as the adjacent column. For example, if you type data in cells A1:A20, type a formula or text in cell B1, press **ENTER**, and then double-click the fill handle. Microsoft Excel fills the data down the column from cell B1 to cell B20.

16.   Custom Auto Fill

By default the Excel auto-fill works great for months and days of the week, in both the abbreviated form like Sun and Mon, or full names like Sunday and Monday.

Let us say you have a need to use auto-fill that is very specific to your need. For instance you could have a list of Sales districts that you need to fill repeatedly, employees in your team, a list of students in your course, or any other custom list that you use frequently.

I am going to list out the steps to create your Custom List with the Excel 2010 Auto Fill feature.

Step 1: Click File, Info, Options

Figure 26

Step 2: Under Options, scroll to Advanced, Edit Custom Lists, and Click OK

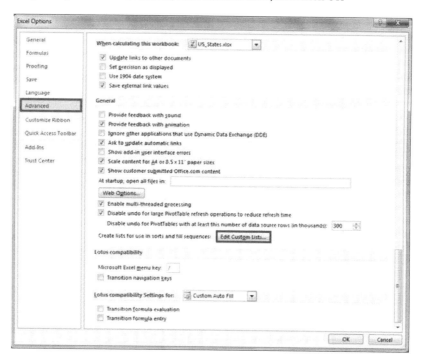

Figure 27

Step 3: Here you have two options – if you have simple data, click Add, and type in the values or click Import, and specify the range for the list.

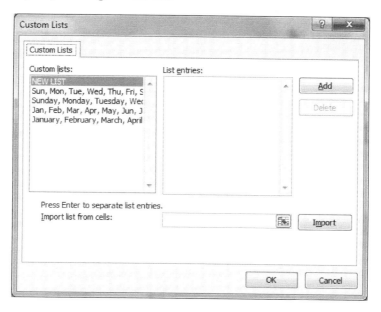

Figure 28

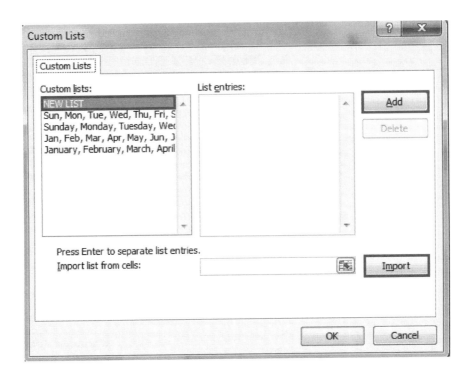

Figure 29

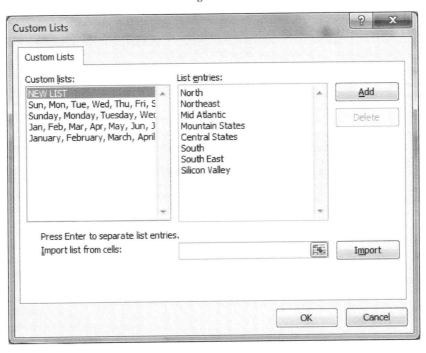

Figure 30

Steps for Import

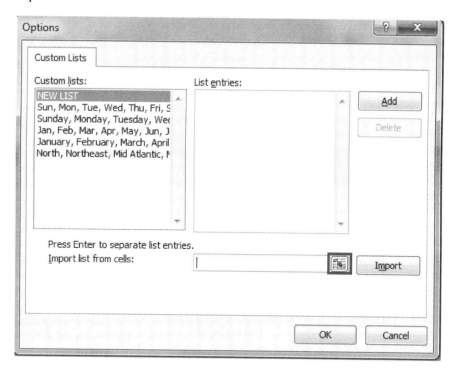

Figure 31

Figure 32

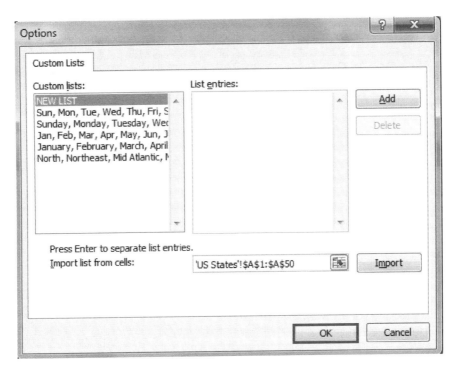

Figure 33

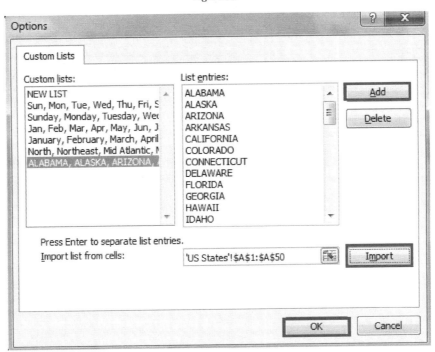

Figure 34

Step 4: Click OK and exit.

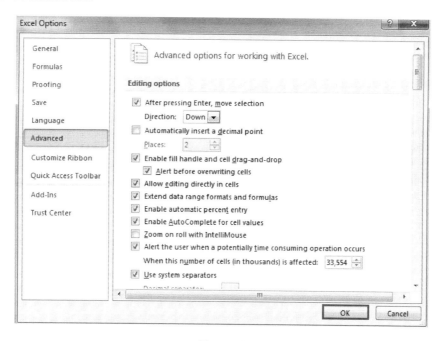

Figure 35

Now when you fill out the series for your sales district or states the Auto Fill works as expected.

Figure 36

Note the Auto Fill list has a limitation of 255 characters, hence in the case of US states it only fills through Nevada. The workaround will be to have a second list, New Hampshire to Wyoming.

17. Fill Weekdays

You can use auto-fill to fill the seven days of the week, since it is prepopulated in Excel. However there might be times you want to fill just the weekdays, especially if you are trying to make a coverage call schedule for a clinic or reporting schedule. One way is to fill the weekdays and delete the weekend days. It would work, but there is a better way. Here is how:

Step 1: Fill in any two cells you want to fill the weekdays in. In this example, Cell A1 and A2.

Step 2: Select those two cells and right click the mouse, then drag the fill handle and release. The Pop Up Menu will show an option to fill weekdays.

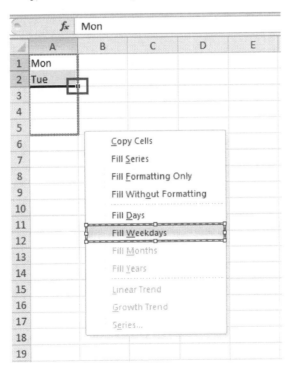

Figure 37

The output will appear like the figure below. Note that the weekends are missing.

Figure 38

18. Quick Close

Double-click on the Microsoft Excel Icon to close Microsoft Excel.

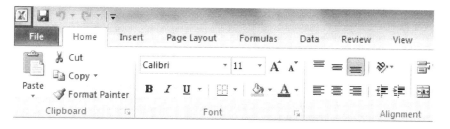

Figure 39

It's that simple. The dialog displays "Do you want to save the changes you made to "YourFileName.xlsx?"

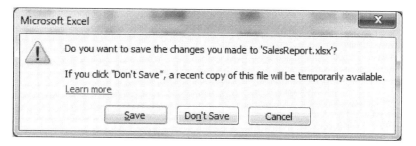

Figure 40

19.   Freeze Panes

This command can save time in your day-to-day work and improve productivity, especially with large spreadsheets. Let us say you have a spreadsheet with 60 rows and 10 columns. The moment you start scrolling across, you may forget the column or row label and have to scroll back and forth to make sure you are editing the right cell. The solution is **Freeze Panes**. Here is how it works.

Let us say you have this spreadsheet:

	Month	Year	Category	Salesperson	Region	Sales		Units	Discount	OrderType
1	**Month**	Year	Category	Salesperson	Region	Sales		Units	Discount	OrderType
2	January	2001	Automotive	Ken	West	$	7,289	30	18%	Web
3	February	2001	Electronics	Dan	East	$	7,249	16	15%	Retail
4	March	2001	Automotive	Jan	East	$	7,212	5	19%	Wholesale
5	April	2001	Apparel	Brian	South	$	7,172	72	19%	Retail
6	May	2001	Childrens	Andy	North	$	7,110	58	16%	Retail
7	June	2001	Home	Karen	East	$	6,996	182	19%	Retail
8	July	2001	Garden	Ryan	West	$	6,973	150	18%	Web
9	August	2001	Tools	Sachin	East	$	6,971	188	20%	Retail
10	September	2001	Electronics	Amitabh	East	$	6,868	185	16%	Retail
11	October	2001	Toys	Kris	North	$	6,806	156	19%	Web
12	November	2001	Automotive	Dey	West	$	6,744	186	18%	Wholesale
13	December	2003	Electronics	Taylor	South	$	6,373	175	14%	Wholesale
14	January	2001	Automtive	Tom	North	$	6,361	202	19%	Phone
15	February	2005	Apparel	Karen	East	$	6,227	159	19%	Phone
16	March	2001	Childrens	Ken	West	$	6,215	190	15%	Phone
17	April	2001	Home	Karen	East	$	6,167	176	8%	Web
18	May	2002	Garden	Taylor	South	$	6,149	140	19%	Retail
19	June	2001	Tools	Brian	South	$	6,111	188	14%	Retail
20	July	2001	Electronics	Kory	South	$	6,080	189	19%	Web
21	August	2001	Toys	Ken	West	$	5,949	151	13%	Phone
22	September	2001	Automotive	Brian	South	$	5,842	80	18%	Phone
23	October	2001	Electronics	Dan	East	$	5,828	188	16%	Wholesale
24	November	2001	Automotive	George	North	$	5,825	138	16%	Phone
25	December	2001	Apparel	Patricia	West	$	5,807	185	14%	Phone
26	January	2001	Childrens	Ken	West	$	5,768	131	15%	Phone
27	February	2001	Home	Amitabh	East	$	5,764	179	15%	Retail

Figure 41

The monitor's window can only accommodate say, 30 rows:

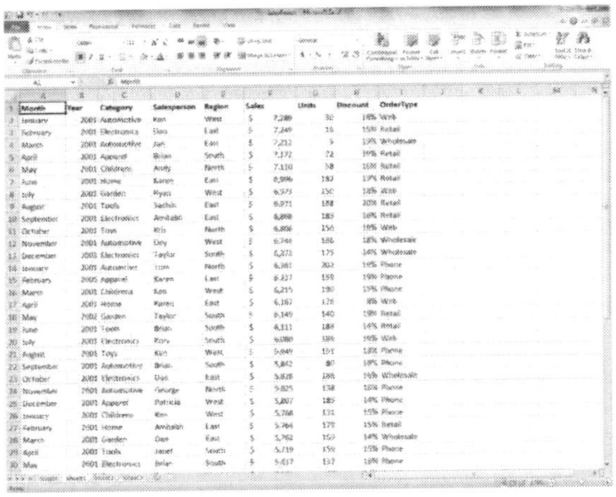

Figure 42

The moment you scroll down to row 33 or higher, you will lose sight of the column labels. To avoid that from happening, freeze the top row:

Step 1 – Put your cursor where you want it, usually cell B2 to freeze both the columns and rows
Step 2 - Click on the **View** tab
Step 3 – Go to **Freeze Panes** and select an option. You can freeze both rows and columns or just top rows or just the first columns, depending on where the cursor is.

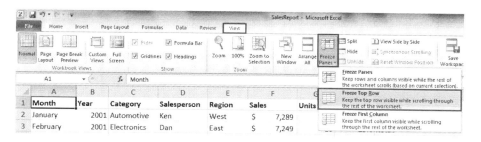

Figure 43

20. Moving sheets

Let us say you have a spreadsheet that contains your work and you are collating the work across teams. A common scenario is for everyone on a team of ten to send their vacation and annual projects plans to one person to compile it into one final workbook.

One way might be to copy the sheets one-by-one. The other is to move the sheets altogether. Here we have two workbooks open side by side:

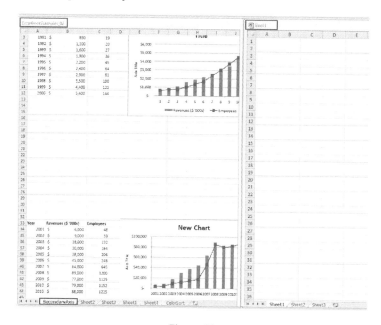

Figure 44

Let us say we have to move the sheet called *SecondaryAxis* over to **Book1.**

To move the sheet, right click on the tab name of the sheet you want to move (in the source workbook) as shown below – "Secondary Axis", and click on **Move or Copy:**

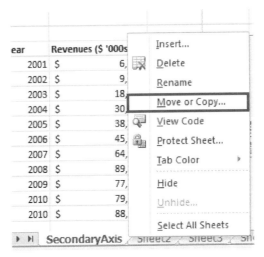

Figure 45

That will reveal three options under **To Book:**

Move it to another open book.
Move it to the same book, at some other position.
Move it to a new book.

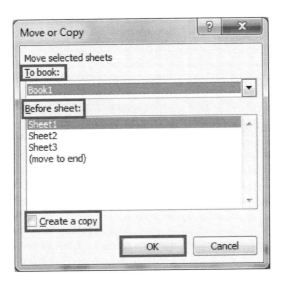

Figure 46

If you don't want to move it, you can just create a copy and the original book is saved as is. In our example the final product looks like this in Book 1:

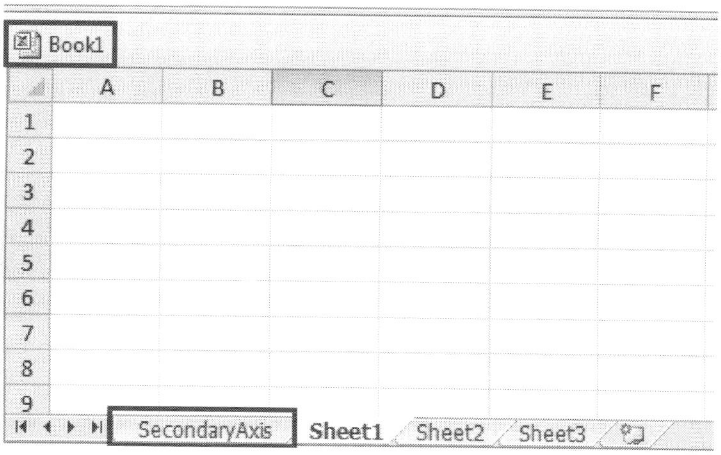

Figure 47

Data Management

21. Hide and Unhide Sheet

Often when working on group projects or monthly or yearly planning reports, you end up with various versions of work tabs for different scenarios. When you are sharing the spreadsheet with your team member you may want to keep all tabs in the same spreadsheet (so that you are not maintaining versions of your work in different places), yet show only the active tabs to your team members.

Fortunately, Excel provides a cool feature called **Hide Worksheet**. Only you know that your original versions are "hidden" and you can refer to them anytime. It is better than password-protected sheets since most often everyone should have access to the raw data if they need to.

Hiding a particular tab or spreadsheet is pretty simple:

Step 1 - Click on **Format** in the **Home** Tab

Figure 48

Step 2 - Click on **Hide and Unhide** under Visibility
Step 3 - Select **Hide Sheet**

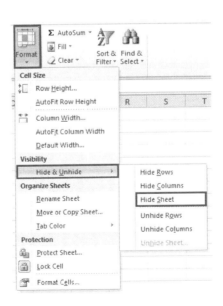

Figure 49

Step 4 - The active sheet will be hidden

You can hide multiple sheets by holding down the **Ctrl key** and selecting multiple tabs at one time.

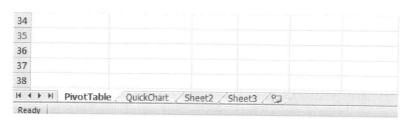

Figure 50

If you want to unhide:

Step 1 - Go to any sheet
Step 2 - Click on **Format** in the **Home** tab

Figure 51

Step 3- Under **Visibility** select **Hide & Unhide**
Step 4 - Click on **Unhide Sheet**

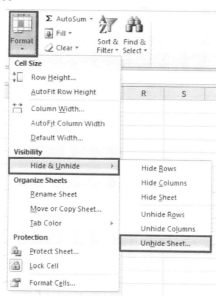

Figure 52

On clicking it will launch a window of all hidden sheets in this case, for example, sales data.

Unhide
Unhide sheet:
SalesData
OK
Cancel

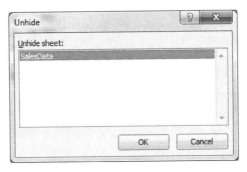

Figure 53

Step 5 - Click **OK** and the sheet will appear

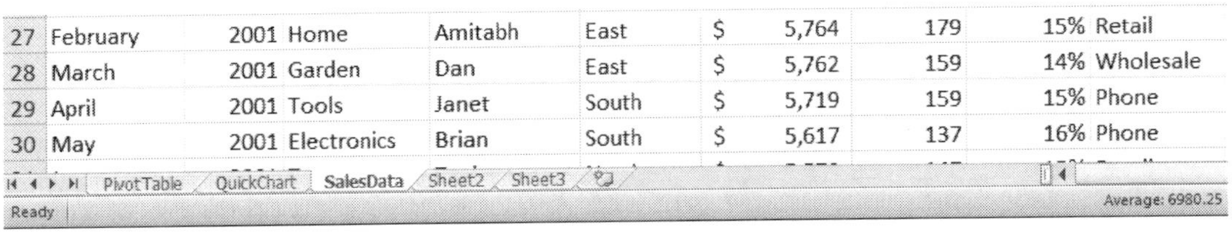

27 February 2001 Home Amitabh East $ 5,764 179 15% Retail
28 March 2001 Garden Dan East $ 5,762 159 14% Wholesale
29 April 2001 Tools Janet South $ 5,719 159 15% Phone
30 May 2001 Electronics Brian South $ 5,617 137 16% Phone
PivotTable
QuickChart
SalesData
Sheet2
Sheet3
Ready
Average: 6980.25

Figure 54

The other way to hide and unhide a spreadsheet is to right-click on the tab of an active sheet and click on **Hide**.

Insert...
Delete
Rename
Move or Copy...
View Code
Protect Sheet...
Tab Color
Hide
Unhide...
Select All Sheets

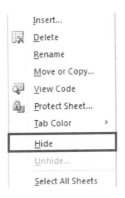

Figure 55

To unhide, right-click on any other active sheet and click **Unhide**

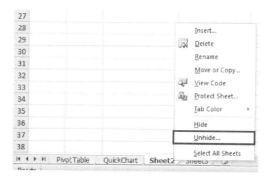

Figure 56

If you don't want to hide a whole worksheet:

To hide the current row, **press ctrl+9**
To hide the current column, **press ctrl+0**

22.   Faster Data Entry

Let us say you have a spreadsheet that lists some of the United States cities and some entries for events scheduled by your company. When you want to enter any new data, Excel automatically shows an entry corresponding to the first letter of the word you want to type. However if you click on **ALT+Down Arrow,** Excel will give you options to enter the values in the column in the alphabetic order. In the example below if I select Houston and click the Cell A17 the value of the cell will show Houston. This is very useful if you have a lot of values with the same name or if the values are hard to remember such as spare part codes or registration numbers.

Figure 57

23. Sorting

Sorting is a basic command in Microsoft Excel and can be a powerful tool in helping you analyze your data by sorting alphabetically, or by high to low, or by a custom sort that you define. You can sort on any column. Here are the basics:

Step 1 – Select your data, then click on **Data** and **Sort**.

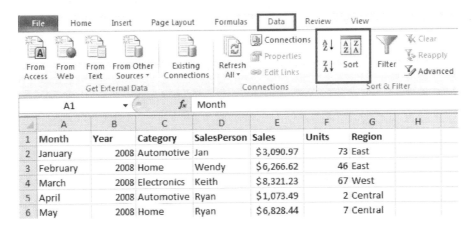

Figure 58

Step 2 - If your data has header rows that you don't want included in the sort, for instance the column labels, just check the box to let Microsoft Excel know to exclude that row from the sorting exercise. If you want multiple levels of sorting, click on Custom Sort, and **Add Level**. In this case, first we are sorting on Category, and within Category we are sorting by Sales.

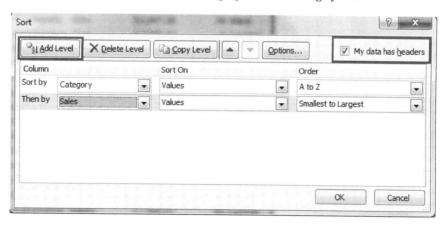

Figure 59

You can experiment with the various options and set your own sorting criteria. Sort may be the best command to accomplish multi-level sorting of data.

24. Sorting by Color

Now this one is one of my favorites. A lot of experienced users may roll their eyes on the sorting command as too basic. However, as I have mentioned, given the broad use of Excel in text management, it is likely you run into a lot of data that is mixed and may need to be aggregated based on context, and not alphabetical or numeric value.

Let us say we have a sales and marketing plan for a company that has several rows of content.

	A	B	C	D
1	**Planned Activity**	**Detail**	**Timing**	**Region**
2	Sales	Training for the sales force	Q1-Q4	All
3	Partner	Training for the partners	Q1	All
4	Demos	Online demo	Q2	All
5	Demos	Demo Laptops for the field sales force	Q1	All
6	Demos	Partner ready customizable demo	Q3	All
7	Sales	Incentive Plan	Q3	All
8	Marketing Brochures	Online Web downloadable	Q1	All
9	Marketing Brochures	Partner print ready brochures	Q2	All
10	Marketing Brochures	Salesforce print ready brochures	Q2	All
11	Marketing	Online campign	Q1	All
12	Marketing	Email campaign	Q1	All
13	Marketing	Web banner acquisition	Q2	All
14	In person Event	Sales	Q3	East
15	In person Event	Partner	Q4	West
16				

Figure 60

Now if we need to sort this data so that we have separate items for Sales, Partners, and Online, we might actually highlight each of them in a unique color, so that if we want to see all activities that are, say, related to the Online campaign, we can view them at a glance like shown below:

	A	B	C	D
1	**Planned Activity**	**Detail**	**Timing**	**Region**
2	Sales	Training for the sales force	Q1-Q4	All
3	Partner	Training for the partners	Q1	All
4	Demos	Online demo	Q2	All
5	Demos	Demo Laptops for the field sales force	Q1	All
6	Demos	Partner ready customizable demo	Q3	All
7	Sales	Incentive Plan	Q3	All
8	Marketing Brochures	Online Web downloadable	Q1	All
9	Marketing Brochures	Partner print ready brochures	Q2	All
10	Marketing Brochures	Salesforce print ready brochures	Q2	All
11	Marketing	Online campign	Q1	All
12	Marketing	Email campaign	Q1	All
13	Marketing	Web banner acquisition	Q2	All
14	In person Event	Sales	Q3	East
15	In person Event	Partner	Q4	West

Figure 61

So now we know at a glance all the activities that are highlighted in green are sales-related activities, those highlighted in yellow are online activities and those in blue are partner-related.

This is ok if the number of activities are few, but imagine if you had 100 or 200 rows and it becomes difficult to process the information. What if you could sort the same info by color? Fortunately, Excel makes it easy. Here are the steps to follow:

Step 1 – Select the data, in this case Cell A1 through cell D15, and select **Data, Sort**

Figure 62

Step 2 – Select **Planned Activity** for **Sort By,** and select **Cell Color** in the **Sort On** option:

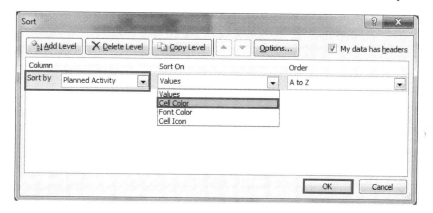

Figure 63

You will get an option to choose the color sort order. Please make sure to add **Add Level** for each color.

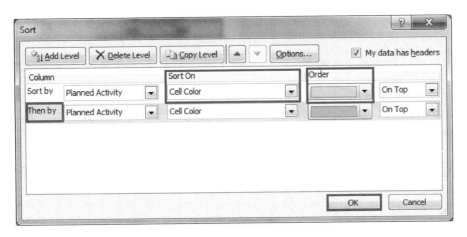

Figure 64

Step 3 – Click **OK.** The output is sorted by color.

	A	B	C	D
1	**Planned Activity**	**Detail**	**Timing**	**Region**
2	Demos	Online demo	Q2	All
3	Marketing Brochures	Online Web downloadable	Q1	All
4	Marketing	Online campign	Q1	All
5	Marketing	Email campaign	Q1	All
6	Marketing	Web banner acquisition	Q2	All
7	Partner	Training for the partners	Q1	All
8	Demos	Partner ready customizable demo	Q3	All
9	Marketing Brochures	Partner print ready brochures	Q2	All
10	In person Event	Partner	Q4	West
11	Sales	Training for the sales force	Q1-Q4	All
12	Demos	Demo Laptops for the field sales force	Q1	All
13	Sales	Incentive Plan	Q3	All
14	Marketing Brochures	Salesforce print ready brochures	Q2	All
15	In person Event	Sales	Q3	East

Figure 65

25.   Remove Duplicates

Let us say you have customer records from your company's sales transactions and you want to see how many unique customers you have and you want to get rid of the duplicates.

Here is the sample set:

	A	B	C	D	E
1	**Customer ID**	**Customer Name**	**City**	**State**	**Transaction Amount**
2	176694	Cindy Johnson	New York	NY	$ 3,326.00
3	916613	Jon Abernathy	Rochester	NY	$ 385.00
4	183410	Malcolm Marshall	Miami	FL	$ 5,175.00
5	511794	Allan Donald	Dallas	TX	$ 3,364.00
6	267511	Wasim Akram	Phoenix	AZ	$ 1,260.00
7	335004	Rick Darling	Los Angel	CA	$ 6,314.00
8	778930	Michael Holding	Atlanta	GA	$ 4,850.00
9	441635	April DeVenuto	New York	NY	$ 6,104.00
10	438157	Justin Langer	Baltimore	MD	$ 9,894.00
11	697179	Cathy Slater	Des Moine	IA	$ 4,780.00
12	477548	Brooke Hayden	Denver	CO	$ 7,459.00
13	183410	Malcolm Marshall	Miami	FL	$ 6,229.00
14	267511	Wasim Akram	Phoenix	AZ	$ 8,069.00
15	778930	Michael Holding	Atlanta	GA	$ 9,786.00
16	438157	Justin Langer	Baltimore	MD	$ 9,180.00
17	477548	Brooke Hayden	Denver	CO	$ 9,922.00
18	916613	Jon Abernathy	Rochester	NY	$ 142.00
19					

Figure 66

I can see some customers are repeated a few times in the database, since they have multiple transactions. I could sort by Customer ID and then count the distinct customer ID's, but what if I had a query on how many unique customers we have, instead? Excel makes it easier.

Step 1 – Select the data and go to **Data, Remove Duplicates**

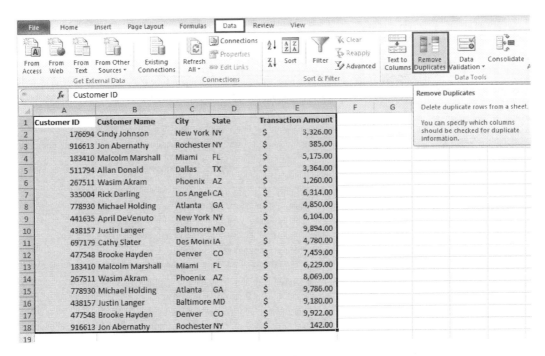

Figure 67

You will get a pop-up where you can select what combination of unique values you want. I just unchecked the Transaction Amount. If I wanted the unique city or unique state I would just check that box. Be a bit cautious – it is easier to take more out, than to add back.

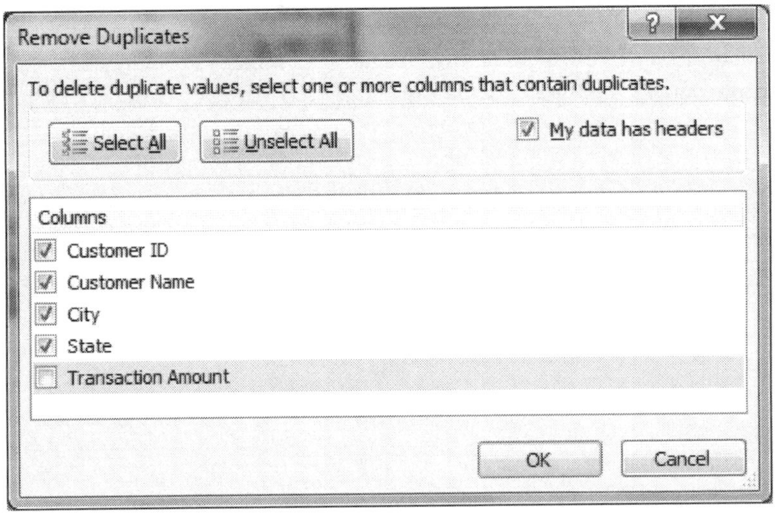

Figure 68

When you click OK Excel tells you the number of duplicate rows removed.

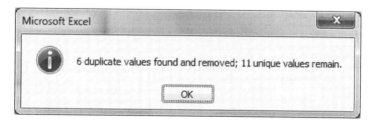

Figure 69

This is what the final output looks like.

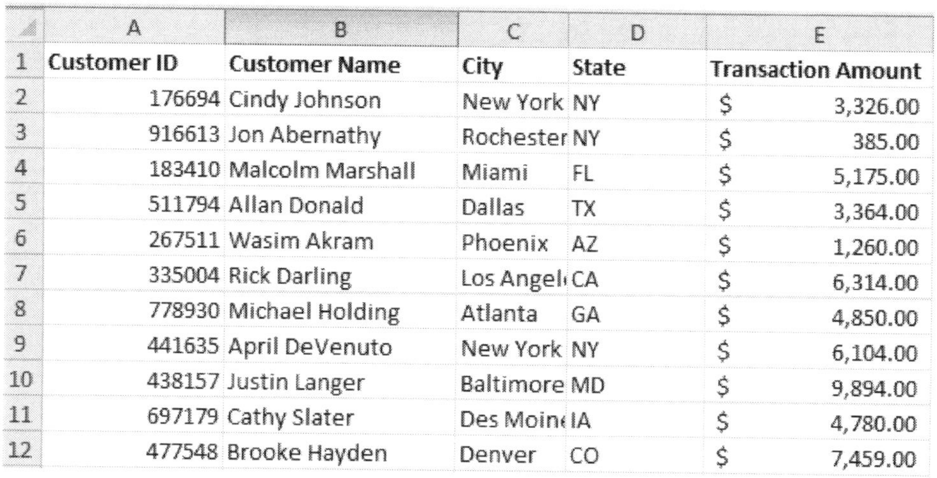

	A	B	C	D	E
1	**Customer ID**	**Customer Name**	**City**	**State**	**Transaction Amount**
2	176694	Cindy Johnson	New York	NY	$ 3,326.00
3	916613	Jon Abernathy	Rochester	NY	$ 385.00
4	183410	Malcolm Marshall	Miami	FL	$ 5,175.00
5	511794	Allan Donald	Dallas	TX	$ 3,364.00
6	267511	Wasim Akram	Phoenix	AZ	$ 1,260.00
7	335004	Rick Darling	Los Angel(	CA	$ 6,314.00
8	778930	Michael Holding	Atlanta	GA	$ 4,850.00
9	441635	April DeVenuto	New York	NY	$ 6,104.00
10	438157	Justin Langer	Baltimore	MD	$ 9,894.00
11	697179	Cathy Slater	Des Moin(	IA	$ 4,780.00
12	477548	Brooke Hayden	Denver	CO	$ 7,459.00

Figure 70

26.   Conditional Formatting

You will love this. Let's assume you have a lot of data and you quickly want to see some values visually. The best tool to do this with is conditional formatting. In regard to the table above, if you want to know the most expensive items versus least expensive, you can do the following:

Step 1 - Select the column
Step 2 - Click on **Conditional Formatting** on the **Home** tab

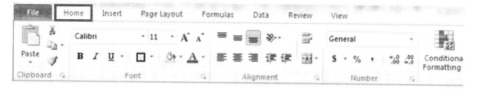

Figure 71

Step 3 - Click on the down arrow and make a selection

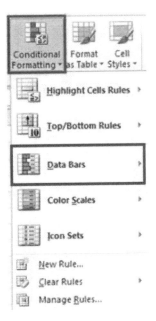

Figure 72

In the example below, I selected **Data Bars**. Isn't this cool?

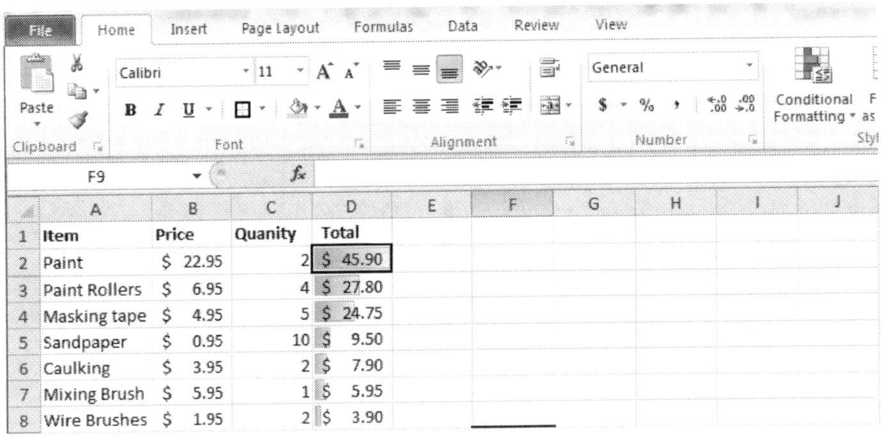

Figure 73

If you select **Icon Sets**, the view changes to:

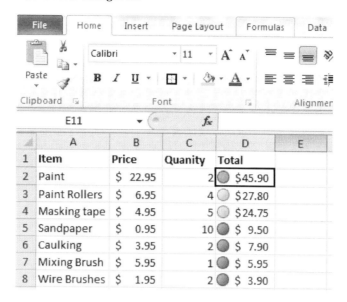

Figure 74

Now you can quickly see the items less than $10.

45

27. Transpose - Convert Rows to Columns or Vice Versa

Let's say someone sent you a spreadsheet with the data laid out as follows, with months going across and all subsequent information like "SalesPerson" and "Sales" also going across.

Figure 75

If you instead prefer to consume the information with months going down the rows, you could use **Transpose**. It is a very handy feature. Here is how it works:

Step 1 - Select all the cells you want to transpose

Figure 76

Step 2 - Copy cells (or click CTRL+C)
Step 3 - Go to the first empty cell
Step 4 - Right-click and Select **Paste Special**
Step 5 - Select **Transpose**

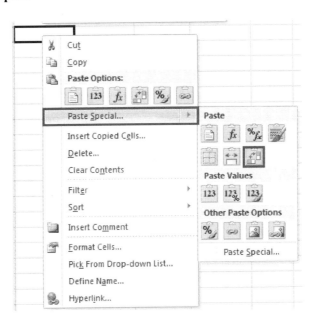

Figure 77

You can select from either the fourth option under **Paste Options** or the **Transpose** from the pop-out menu under **Paste**.

Step 5 - Your data is now converted into your desired format: ta-da! Imagine how long this would take if you tried transposing cell by cell.

	A	B	C	D	E	F	G	H	I
1	**Month**	January	February	March	April	May	June	July	August
2	**Year**	2001	2001	2001	2001	2001	2001	2001	2001
3	**Category**	Automotive	Electronics	Automotive	Apparel	Childrens	Home	Garden	Tools
4	**Salesperson**	Ken	Dan	Jan	Brian	Andy	Karen	Ryan	Sachin
5	**Sales**	$ 7,289	$ 7,249	$ 7,212	$7,172	$ 7,110	$6,996	$6,973	$6,971
6									
7	**Month**	Year		Category	Salesperson	Sales			
8	January	2001	Automotive	Ken	$7,289				
9	February	2001	Electronics	Dan	$7,249				
10	March	2001	Automotive	Jan	$7,212				
11	April	2001	Apparel	Brian	$7,172				
12	May	2001	Childrens	Andy	$7,110				
13	June	2001	Home	Karen	$6,996				
14	July	2001	Garden	Ryan	$6,973				
15	August	2001	Tools	Sachin	$6,971				
16	September	2001	Electronics	Amitabh	$6,868				
17	October	2001	Toys	Kris	$6,806				
18	November	2001	Automotive	Dey	$6,744				
19	December	2003	Electronics	Taylor	$6,373				
20	January	2001	Automtive	Tom	$6,361				
21	February	2005	Apparel	Karen	$6,227				
22	March	2001	Childrens	Ken	$6,215				
23	April	2001	Home	Karen	$6,167				
24	May	2002	Garden	Taylor	$6,149				
25	June	2001	Tools	Brian	$6,111				
26	July	2001	Electronics	Kory	$6,080				
27	August	2001	Toys	Ken	$5,949				
28	September	2001	Automotive	Brian	$5,842				
29	October	2001	Electronics	Dan	$5,828				
30	November	2001	Automotive	George	$5,825				
31	December	2001	Apparel	Patricia	$5,807				
32	January	2001	Childrens	Ken	$5,768				
33	February	2001	Home	Amitabh	$5,764				
34	March	2001	Garden	Dan	$5,762				
35									
36									

Figure 78

28. Filter

Sometimes in large data sets you want to view only a subset of the data or you need to filter the data based on your criteria. In the example below, if I want to sort all the records that are in New York (NY), here are the steps:

Step 1 – Go to **Data, Filter**

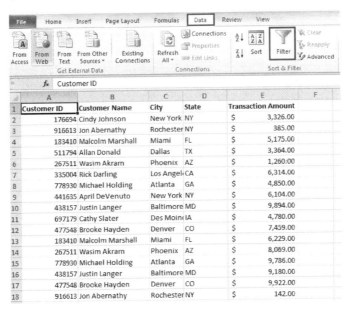

Figure 79

Step 2 – Click on the Dropdown arrow next to state and uncheck the box (Select All) and Select only NY and click OK

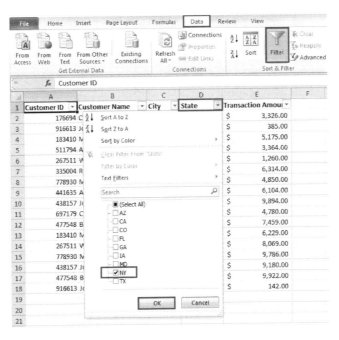

Figure 80

The output is as follows:

	A	B	C	D	E
1	Customer ID	Customer Name	City	State	Transaction Amou
2	176694	Cindy Johnson	New York	NY	$ 3,326.00
3	916613	Jon Abernathy	Rochester	NY	$ 385.00
9	441635	April DeVenuto	New York	NY	$ 6,104.00
18	916613	Jon Abernathy	Rochester	NY	$ 142.00
19					

Figure 81

Note: To quickly activate the filter, just type in **CTRL+SHIFT+L**

Some of the other options you should explore on your own are Text Filters, such as "Equals NY" or "Begins with New" which will return New York and New Jersey.

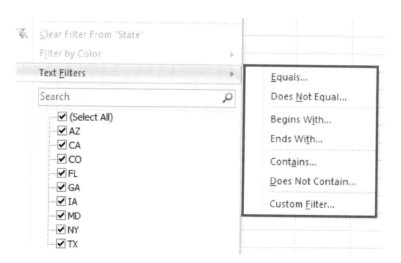

Figure 82

Data Validation

29.   Create a drop-down list

Sometimes you want data integrity in a spreadsheet so that it is easier to track, manage and report on the underlying data. Hence, if you want people to enter a state for all sales in the New York stores, you may find yourself with entries like NY, Newyork, New York, etc. Chances are, in some of the cases, the user had a keyboard error or used the state abbreviation. Excel provides a really easy way to prevent such occurrences.

Let us say you are ordering food for your team offsite. You ask the folks to enter their options. You want to restrict options to 4 possible choices: Chinese, Mexican, Vegetarian, and Special diet. Here are the steps:

Step 1 – Create your list with the available food choices as shown below in cells G2-G5:

	A	B	C	D	E	F	G	H	I
1	Name	Food Preference					Available Food Preferences		
2	Alistair						Chinese		
3	Michael						Mexican		
4	Andrew						Vegetarian		
5	Belinda						Special diet		
6	Kevin								
7	Eoin								
8	Ravinder								
9	Graham								
10	Stuart								
11	Wendy								
12	Karen								
13									
14									

Figure 83

Step 2 – To make a drop down list applicable to the people in Cells B2-B12, move the cursor to cell B2

Step 3 – Go to Data, Data Validation, Data Validation (note the repetition)

Figure 84

Step 4 – On the settings tab enter the criteria. Choose Allow – List, specify the source by either entering the source list values or selecting the list from the icon. Click OK.

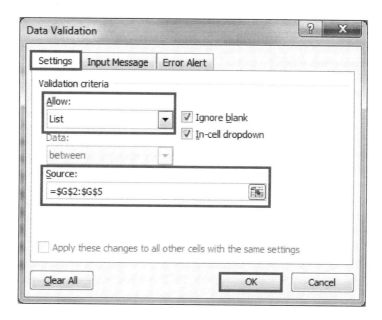

Figure 85

Step 5 – Drag the anchor all the way to B12. Your drop down list is ready. The cell anchor can be identified by a dark square at the bottom of the active or selected cell.

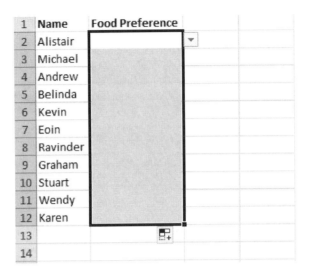

Figure 86

Now when you go to enter the data in the cells you will see the options from the choices you have defined in the list.

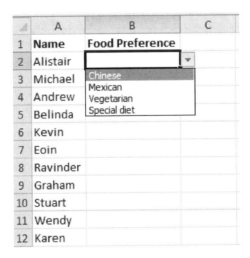

Figure 87

Tip: one way to ensure that no one changes the master list is to hide the column with the list. This works in simple lists. In more advanced spreadsheets you might want to use cell protection.

30. Add a dialog on Data Entry

Let us say in the example above someone wants to add Italian food as an option. To prevent an unpleasant user experience, it might be a good option to add a dialog at the time of data entry.

Step 1 – Go to **Data, Data Validation, Data Validation**. Select **Error Alert.** Choose the style and the title of the error box and the Error message. Click OK.

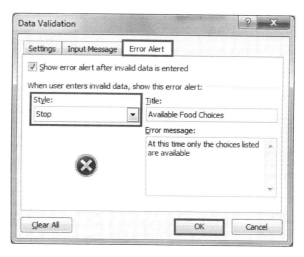

Figure 88

Now when a user enters an invalid data the user will get a prompt.

Figure 89

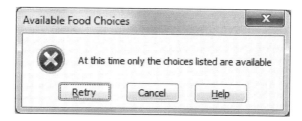

Figure 90

Formulas

31. View All Formulas at Once

When working on projects, we might often get a spreadsheet or workbook to review that has been programmed by a colleague. To view all the formulas on the spreadsheet just enter **CTRL and "~"** (the tilde symbol).

Here's an example:

	A	B	C	D	E	F	G	H
1		Sales 2008	Sales 2009	Growth				
2	North	$ 100,000.00	$ 120,000.00	20.00%				
3	East	$ 223,000.00	$ 241,000.00	8.07%				
4	South	$ 314,000.00	$ 342,000.00	8.92%				
5	West	$ 93,000.00	$ 108,000.00	16.13%				
6	**Total**	**$ 730,000.00**	**$ 811,000.00**	**11.10%**				
7								

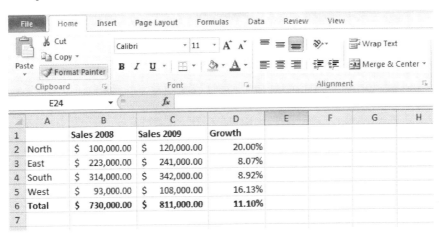

Figure 91

To see the formula view, hit **CTL + "~"** within the spreadsheet. To go back, hit **CTRL+ "~"** again.

	A	B	C	D
1		Sales 2008	Sales 2009	Growth
2	North	100000	120000	=(C2-B2)/B2
3	East	223000	241000	=(C3-B3)/B3
4	South	314000	342000	=(C4-B4)/B4
5	West	93000	108000	=(C5-B5)/B5
6	**Total**	**=SUM(B2:B5)**	**=SUM(C2:C5)**	**=(C6-B6)/B6**
7				

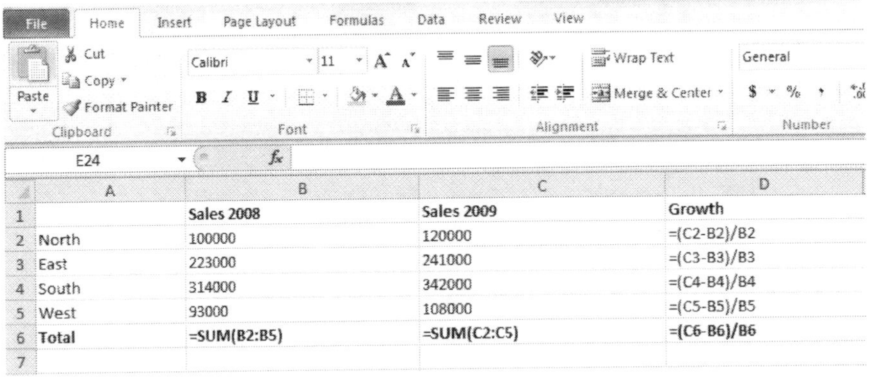

Figure 92

32.   Absolute Reference

Let us say you have a data set like the one below where you have the sales of various products and you want to calculate the percentage each product contributes to the bottom line. The formula is simple.

Percentage of total Sales for each product = (Sales for that product/Total Sales) An example: In cell C2 below, you would type this formula: =118,719/2,087,757.   And if you format the cell C2 as a percentage, it automatically shows the resulting values as percentages.

	fx =B2/B9	

	A	B	C
1	Product	Annual Sales ($)	Percentage of Total Sales
2	Product A	$ 118,719	5.7%
3	Product B	$ 511,535	
4	Product C	$ 162,854	
5	Product D	$ 334,112	
6	Product E	$ 335,787	
7	Product F	$ 476,976	
8	Product G	$ 147,774	
9	Total Sales	$ 2,087,757	

Figure 93

Now one way to fill all the percentages for all of the other products is to manually enter the formula for each cell, which is painful. The other way is to drag C2's fill handle down until C8, and the formula is copied for each cell. But when we do this, the formula for Cell C3 changes to B3/B10 and for C4 it is B4/B11 etc. Hence we get error values. We need for all of these to be divided by Total Sales in cell B9.

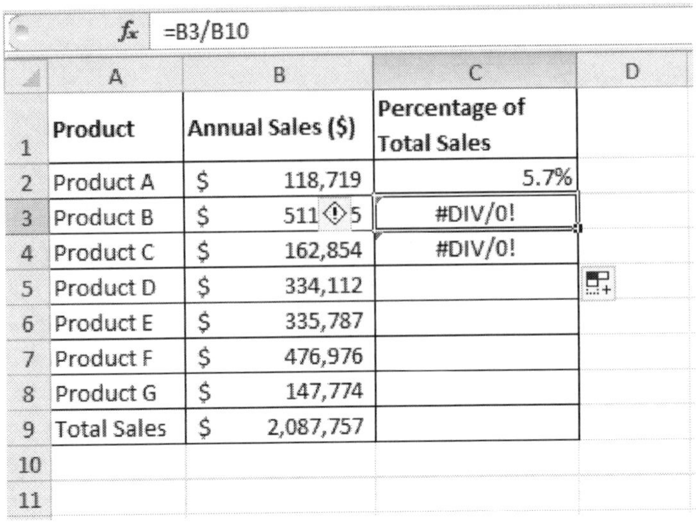

	fx	=B3/B10		
	A	B	C	D
1	Product	Annual Sales ($)	Percentage of Total Sales	
2	Product A	$ 118,719	5.7%	
3	Product B	$ 511◇5	#DIV/0!	
4	Product C	$ 162,854	#DIV/0!	
5	Product D	$ 334,112		
6	Product E	$ 335,787		
7	Product F	$ 476,976		
8	Product G	$ 147,774		
9	Total Sales	$ 2,087,757		
10				
11				

Figure 94

While we want the numerator to change we want the denominator to be constant or absolute.

There are two ways to achieve the result. Either you enter the actual value for the total sales in the denominator instead of referencing B9, or you make cell B9 absolute, so that when you drag Cell C2's fill handle, the anchor B9 does not change. To achieve this, just edit the formula in cell C2 as:

C2=B2/B$9

All I did was appended a $ sign before the number 9. This tells Excel that the row 9 is fixed. If you wanted to make the column fixed, too, you could make the formula C2=B2/$B$9.

Now when you drag the cells down using C2's fill handle, you get the correct percentages. As you see below in cell C9, the value is 100%.

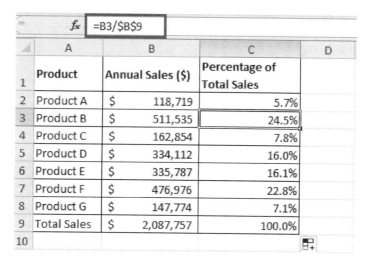

	A	B	C	D
1	Product	Annual Sales ($)	Percentage of Total Sales	
2	Product A	$ 118,719	5.7%	
3	Product B	$ 511,535	24.5%	
4	Product C	$ 162,854	7.8%	
5	Product D	$ 334,112	16.0%	
6	Product E	$ 335,787	16.1%	
7	Product F	$ 476,976	22.8%	
8	Product G	$ 147,774	7.1%	
9	Total Sales	$ 2,087,757	100.0%	
10				

Figure 95

Quick Tip: To make any value absolute click on the cell value in the formula and hit the F4 key. It makes both the row and column absolute.

33.   Remove the formulas but keep the values

If you have worked on a spreadsheet and you have the final numbers which are based on a lot of formulas that you don't want changed, either you want to lock the formulas or you just want to save the output values.

To achieve this all you do is **Select** the data which is based on formulas and in the new destination **Right click** and select **Paste Special,** Select the third option **Values and Source formatting.**

Figure 96

The output looks like this:

	A	B	C
		fx	5.6864376457605%
1	Product	Annual Sales ($)	Percentage of Total Sales
2	Product A	$ 118,719	5.7%
3	Product B	$ 511,535	24.5%
4	Product C	$ 162,854	7.8%
5	Product D	$ 334,112	16.0%
6	Product E	$ 335,787	16.1%
7	Product F	$ 476,976	22.8%
8	Product G	$ 147,774	7.1%
9	Total Sale	$ 2,087,757	100.0%

Figure 97

Note cell C2 has numbers and not formulas.

34. Remove the numbers but keep the formulas

This is the reverse of the previous tip. In this case you want to just preserve the formulas. For example, if someone gives you a spreadsheet all modeled for the tax calculation for the year and all you want to do is save the formulas and plug in your numbers.

Select the cells and hit **CTRL+G** and click on **Special**

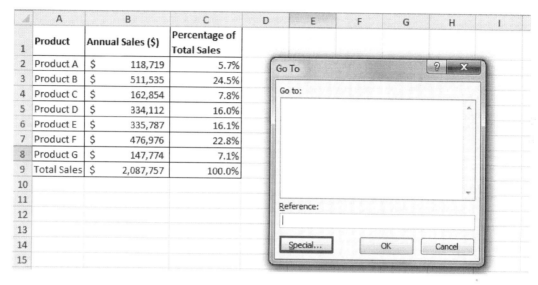

Figure 98

Figure 99

All the cells with the values will be highlighted. Hit **Delete.** Now you have saved the formulas but deleted the values.

	A	B	C	D
1	**Product**	**Annual Sales ($)**	**Percentage of Total Sales**	
2	Product A	$ 118,719	5.7%	
3	Product B	$ 511,535	24.5%	
4	Product C	$ 162,854	7.8%	
5	Product D	$ 334,112	16.0%	
6	Product E	$ 335,787	16.1%	
7	Product F	$ 476,976	22.8%	
8	Product G	$ 147,774	7.1%	
9	Total Sales	$ 2,087,757	100.0%	
10				

fx 118719

Figure 100

In this example you can enter new values for the sales of Product A through Product G and the percentages are calculated easily.

35. Date Calculations

Day Calculator

When working on various projects, you may need to know how many days there are between two given dates so that you can allocate resources accordingly. Even though Microsoft Project is the perfect solution for any project planning work, for most users Microsoft Excel has some really cool functions built in. Have you ever needed to know the number of workdays you have between now and the end of your project?

Networkdays: You can enter two dates in cells B1 and C1. Enter the following in cell D1

=Networkddays(B1,C1). In the below example, we will have 22 weekdays.

A	B	C	D
Work Days in June	6/1/2010	6/30/2010	22

Figure 101

Weekday

To know the day of the week for 6/1 in the preceding figure, instead of looking at the calendar, just type in:
=weekday (cell number with the date in it) in this case: =weekday (B1)
To calculate the value of cell B1, type in the value as shown below:

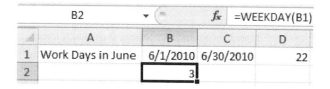

B2		▼	*fx*	=WEEKDAY(B1)

	A	B	C	D
1	Work Days in June	6/1/2010	6/30/2010	22
2		3		

Figure 102

The answer is 3, which means 6/1 falls on a Tuesday, the third day of the week. Sunday is treated as the first day of the week and Saturday the last, and so this goes 1 through 7.

36.   Hide formula Error

Sometimes in a spreadsheet we are faced with formulas that are correct, but the very design of the spreadsheet will cause them to throw an error. Hence for spreadsheets which you know are correctly designed, you may want to suppress the error.

Let us say you have a spreadsheet that captures the inventory of sports goods for a company's store in Maine and you want to know the unit price of each item in the inventory. So in cell D3 we put the formula =B3/C3 to get the unit price per item in the inventory – cell B divided by cell C.

	fx	=B3/C3		

	A	B	C	D
1	Maine Ski Store			
2	Month	Inventory Cost	Quantity	Cost Per Unit
3	Skis	$ 265,958	728	$ 365.3
4	Gloves	$ 183,478	2636	$ 69.6
5	Surfboard	$ -	0	#DIV/0!
6	Snowboards	$ 116,503	706	$ 165.0
7	Shoes	$ 225,776	2521	$ 89.6
8	SunGlasses	$ 165,371	1619	$ 102.1
9	Swimming goggles	$ 1,200	0	#DIV/0!
10	Total	$ 958,286	8210	$ 116.7

Figure 103

Now since this company has a chain of stores and the inventory list is standard, some items like Surfboard show up, and since the store in Maine is the Ski store, it has no Surfboard inventory and so your formula can show an error. To avoid the error showing up, you can modify the formula with an IF and an ISERROR Function:

In cell D3 you can enter =IF(ISERROR(B3/C3),"",B3/C3)

It is a combination of two functions. The way the formula works is if there is an error, ISERROR – it checks for the error condition and returns blank or "" when it encounters an error, else it returns the calculation.

You can replace the empty string with string of your choice. After putting in the function the error looks like this.

	A	B	C	D
		f_x	=IF(ISERROR(B3/C3),"",B3/C3)	
1		Maine Ski Store		
2	Month	Inventory Cost	Quantity	Cost Per Unit
3	Skis	$ 265,958	728	365.3
4	Gloves	$ 183,478	2636	69.6
5	Surfboard	$ -	0	
6	Snowboards	$ 116,503	706	165.0
7	Shoes	$ 225,776	2521	89.6
8	SunGlasses	$ 165,371	1619	102.1
9	Swimming goggles	$ 1,200	0	
10	Total	$ 958,286	8210	$ 116.7

Figure 104

Note the error has been replaced by blank cells.

37. Formula range and Named formulas

Sometimes when we create a formula the logic behind the formula might be clear to the one creating it, but involves some reverse engineering on the part of anyone else to capture the thinking behind it. Wouldn't it be great if we could just use the exact names in the Excel formula so that anyone reading it can quickly understand how the formula was created?

I will illustrate this using an example of an e-mail campaign run by a marketer.

Typical components of an email campaign are the number of e-mails sent out, bounce rate of e-mails, percent of e-mails opened, percent of people clicking on the email link.

The most important metric is actual conversion from the number of e-mails sent, to actual call to action, such as traffic to the webpage or clicks on the Buy Now button to start the purchase.

Here is what the spreadsheet looks like.

	A	B	C
1	**E-mail Campaign Metric**	**Final Numbers**	
2	E-mails Sent	900,000	
3	Bounce Rate	15%	
4	Open Rate	25%	
5	Click Through Rate	8%	
6	Conversion	2700	
7	Net Conversion	0.3%	
8			

Figure 105

If we move the cursor to see the Conversion of the e-mail campaign here is what the formula shows: Cell B6=B2*B3*B4*B5. (See top of illustration below.)

Note: for those using formulas for first time, Excel uses the standard notation: + for addition, - for subtraction, * for multiplication and / for division.

B6	▼	f_x	=B2*B3*B4*B5	
	A	B	C	
1	**E-mail Campaign Metric**	**Final Numbers**		
2	E-mails Sent	900,000		
3	Bounce Rate	15%		
4	Open Rate	25%		
5	Click Through Rate	8%		
6	Conversion	2700		
7	Net Conversion	0.3%		
8				
9				
10				

Figure 106

So, the formula is E-mails Sent * Open Rate * Bounce Rate * Click-Through Rate.

If we edit the formula, we can see the key cells involved. Or, we can see it by giving a user-friendly name to each cell in the formula. Here are the steps.

Step 1 – Move the cursor to cell B2. (See red box in below illustration.) B2 is the name of that cell.

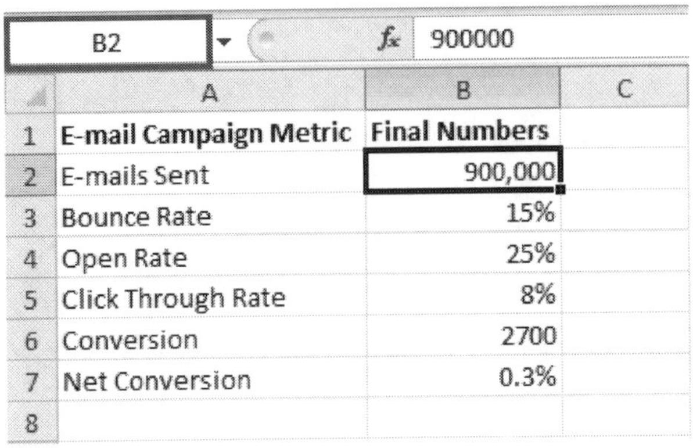

Figure 107

In the Name Box where it shows the cell name, type in a new user-friendly name; in this case we will rename B2 to "Emails_Sent". (See red box in below illustration.)

If you are a new or occasional user of Excel it would be a good idea to review the section in the appendix where the parts of an Excel spreadsheet are illustrated.

As you can see the cell name is now changed to Emails_Sent. Hence, you can refer to either the new cell name or B2 to work with the values contained in the cell.

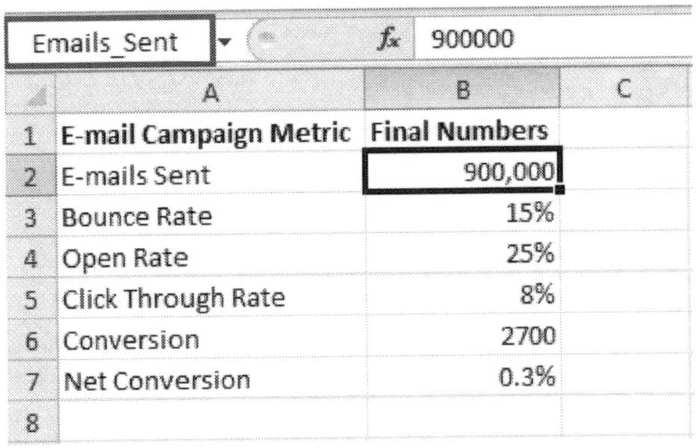

Figure 108

Step 2 – Similarly for cells B3-B6 define the names as follows

> B3 - BounceRate
>
> B4 – OpenRate
>
> B5- ClickThroughRate
>
> B6 - Conversion

Step 3 – Edit the formula to a more readable format

Now in the cell B6 enter the user-friendly formula. Make sure the names are EXACTLY what you have defined in Step 1 and Step 2; "BounceRate" and "Bounce Rate" are treated as two different names.

Conversion		f_x	=Emails_Sent*BounceRate*OpenRate*ClickThroughRate				
	A	B	C	D	E	F	G
1	**E-mail Campaign Metric**	**Final Numbers**					
2	E-mails Sent	900,000					
3	Bounce Rate	15%					
4	Open Rate	25%					
5	Click Through Rate	8%					
6	Conversion	2700					
7	Net Conversion	0.3%					
8							
9							

Figure 109

As you can see the formula now is a lot more reader friendly. Similarly for the Net Conversions the formula is as follows:

Net Conversion = (Conversion/E-mails Sent). It looks like this in the Excel:

B7		f_x	=Conversion/Emails_Sent		
	A	B	C	D	E
1	**E-mail Campaign Metric**	**Final Numbers**			
2	E-mails Sent	900,000			
3	Bounce Rate	15%			
4	Open Rate	25%			
5	Click Through Rate	8%			
6	Conversion	2700			
7	Net Conversion	0.3%			
8					

Figure 110

If you have a lot of names, one way to enter the values is to go to the **Formulas tab,** then **Use in Formulas,** and click on the drop-down arrow. You will see the options of the names available. In this case we can replace B2 with Emails_Sent.

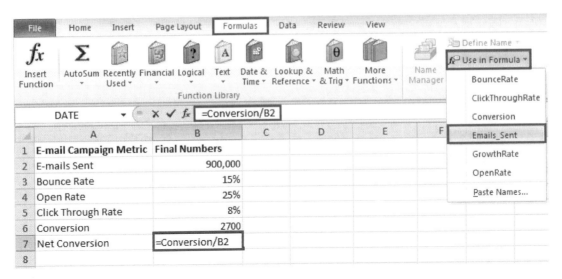

Figure 111

To list all the name ranges in the Excel workbook you can go to **Formulas,** then **Name Manager**

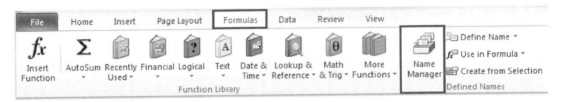

Figure 112

When you click on the **Name Manager** you are prompted with name, value, location and scope of the name. By default all names have a unique scope in the workbook. You can define them to be very specific to the spreadsheet, and you can use the same names in different spreadsheets of a workbook. It can be done at the time of creation in **Formulas, Define Name** and specify the scope. As much as possible, keep it simple and have unique names per workbook.

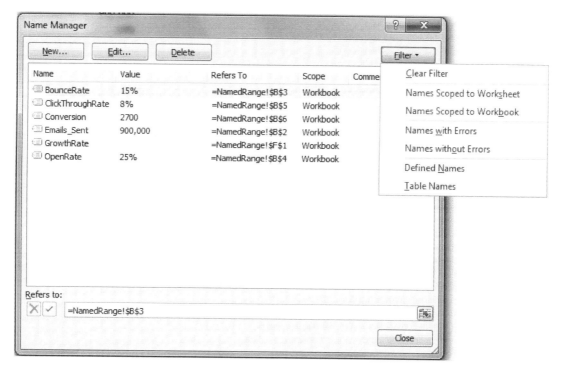

Figure 113

38. Auto Multiply

Let us say you have a pricelist and based on the increase in the cost of gasoline/petrol you want to increase prices by 5%. One option would be to create a formula where you multiply the cells individually using a formula. The other option is **auto multiply**. This is very useful when you have a lot of entries to change. In this case we have an Item list with the prices, and since the prices go up by 5% we enter 1.05 in the new cell.

	A	B	C	D	E
1	Item	Price			
2	Item # 1	$ 3.0		New Price	$ 1.05
3	Item # 2	$ 9.0			
4	Item # 3	$ 8.0			
5	Item # 4	$ 4.0			
6	Item # 5	$ 2.0			
7	Item # 6	$ 2.0			
8	Item # 7	$ 7.0			
9	Item # 8	$ 1.0			
10	Item # 9	$ 1.0			
11	Item # 10	$ 10.0			
12	Item # 11	$ 8.0			
13	Item # 12	$ 1.0			
14	Item # 13	$ 10.0			
15	Item # 14	$ 7.0			
16					

Figure 114

Now to multiply all the cells at the same time without entering a formula for the fear of the formula getting inadvertently changed here are the steps:

Step 1 - Select cell E2, right click and select **Copy**

Step 2 – Next select cells B2 to B15 and right click and select **Paste Special**, **Paste Special** as shown below. A new pop-up menu will show up on the screen.

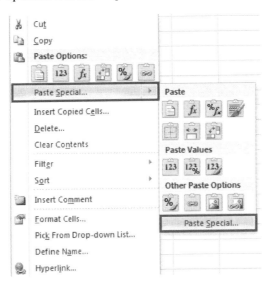

Figure 115

Step 3 – Under Paste, **Select All**, under Operation, choose **Multiply** and click **OK**.

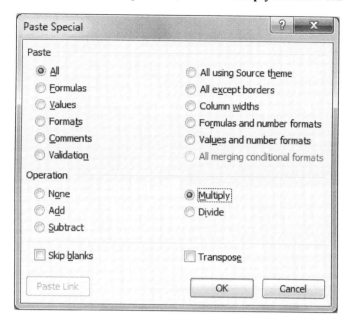

Figure 116

All the selected cell values are multiplied by 1.05 or show an increase of 5%.

	A	B	C	D	E
1	**Item**	**Price**			
2	Item # 1	$ 3.15		New Price	$ 1.05
3	Item # 2	$ 9.45			
4	Item # 3	$ 8.40			
5	Item # 4	$ 4.20			
6	Item # 5	$ 2.10			
7	Item # 6	$ 2.10			
8	Item # 7	$ 7.35			
9	Item # 8	$ 1.05			
10	Item # 9	$ 1.05			
11	Item # 10	$ 10.50			
12	Item # 11	$ 8.40			
13	Item # 12	$ 1.05			
14	Item # 13	$ 10.50			
15	Item # 14	$ 7.35			
16					

Figure 117

39. Protect Formula

Let us say you have a spreadsheet with a formula that you want to protect so that it cannot be changed, such as the sheet below. To protect the cells in the spreadsheet, follow these steps:

	A	B	C	D
		fx	=SUM(B2:B15)	
1	Item	Price		
2	Item # 1	$ 3.15		
3	Item # 2	$ 9.45		
4	Item # 3	$ 8.40		
5	Item # 4	$ 4.20		
6	Item # 5	$ 2.10		
7	Item # 6	$ 2.10		
8	Item # 7	$ 7.35		
9	Item # 8	$ 1.05		
10	Item # 9	$ 1.05		
11	Item # 10	$ 10.50		
12	Item # 11	$ 8.40		
13	Item # 12	$ 1.05		
14	Item # 13	$ 10.50		
15	Item # 14	$ 7.35		
16		$ 76.65		
17				

Figure 118

Step 1 – Go to **Review, Protect Sheet**

Figure 119

Step 2 – Check the box **Protect Sheet and contents of locked cells** and enter password (optional). Click **OK.**

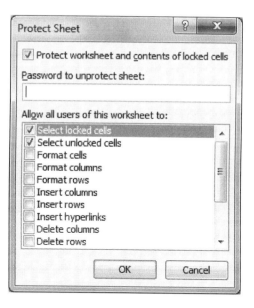

Figure 120

Now your worksheet is protected. Whenyou try to enter data in a locked worksheet you will get this prompt:

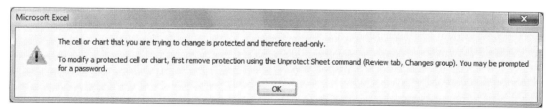

Figure 121

40.   Auditing

This is one of the coolest and most underused tools in Excel. Let us say you are analyzing the sales of an aircraft spare-parts company that supplies parts to major airlines in the United States. You have the sales data shown below. I have deliberately structured the data to show the visualization of the **auditing** tool.

	A	B	C	D	E	F	G	H	I	J	K	L
1	North			South			East			West		
2	City	Sales		City	Sales		City	Sales		City	Sales	
3	Minneapolis	$ 224,414.00		Dallas	$214,117.00		New York	$ 110,659.00		Los Angeles	$121,350.00	
4	Detroit	$ 104,361.00		Lubbock	$ 94,387.00		Boston	$ 112,397.00		Seattle	$ 73,943.00	
5	Chicago	$ 154,933.00		Houston	$197,824.00		Baltimore	$ 242,031.00		Portland	$215,726.00	
6	Total	$ 483,708.00		Baton Rouge	$147,554.00		Miami	$ 146,360.00		SanFrancisco	$101,701.00	
7				Total	$653,882.00		Atlanta	$ 212,046.00		San Diego	$148,889.00	
8							Orlando	$ 235,719.70		Total	$661,609.00	
9							Total	$1,059,212.70				
10												
11	US Sales	$ 2,858,411.70										
12												
13	Key City Sales	$ 724,520.00										
14				Key Index		25.3%						
15												

Figure 122

Now if you received the spreadsheet and you wanted to know how was the **key index** was calculated and what are the **key city sales** made up of, follow these steps:

Step 1 – Go to cell B13 and Select **Formulas**, then **Trace Precedents**

Figure 123

Now you can quickly see which cities contribute to **key city sales**, which in this case are all cities with major airline hubs.

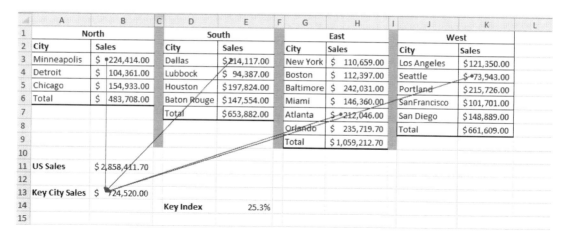

Figure 124

If you want to view which are the cells that depend on or are affected by the value of this cell, select **Formulas, Trace Dependents**. Note the arrow going out from Cell B13 to cell B15.

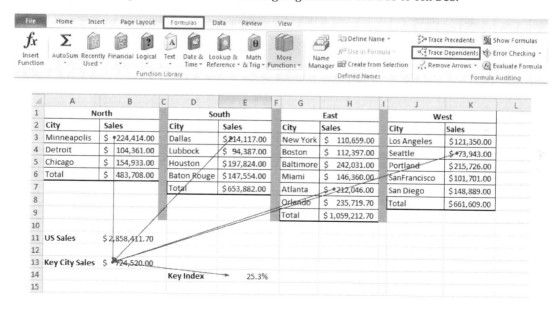

Figure 125

After you are done auditing the sheet, select **Remove Arrows** to go back to the original spreadsheet.

Figure 126

Presentation and Packaging

Let us admit that no matter how good your work is, it is a matter of packaging and presenting that make it appealing to people who are reviewing or seeing your work. Growing up in a country with teachers who always insisted on the core being solid and presentation and packaging being secondary, it required a bit of an adjustment while settling in the United States. While my education provided me with a great foundation, at times I have felt the need to bypass presentation and packaging, which may have hurt my case more often than not.

While most people using Excel tend to be more analytical, a section on presentation and packaging will not hurt!

41. Colored Tabs

Let us start with a basic tip. If you have multiple tabs, you can color code the tabs so that as soon as a user launches the workbook he or she is presented with a very compelling workbook that has various tabs, which are clearly marked by a unique color.

Let us say you have a workbook that has headcount planning and operational expenses of various departments like Sales, Marketing, Support, Engineering, Legal, and Human Resources.

The default spreadsheet looks like this:

Figure 127

To light up the spreadsheet use a different color for each tab. Just right click on the tab that you want to change and move the mouse to change the color.

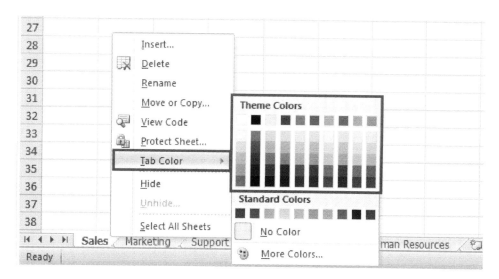

Figure 128

Here is what our spreadsheet looks like. It's a very simple but effective tip to get you on your way to packaging and presenting your final work.

Figure 129

42. Cell Styles

There is another little-used feature in Excel that can really light up a workbook. It is called **Cell Style**. There are several pre-formatted cell styles you can use to beautify your tables, column and row headings. To use Cell Styles go to **Home, Cell Styles**.

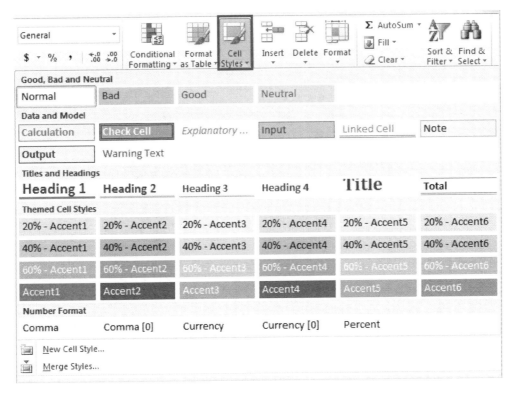

Figure 130

Here is a spreadsheet before and after applying the cell styles.

BEFORE

	A	B	C	D	E
1	Web				
2					
3	Month	Traffic	Conversion	Average Per uniit	Sales ($)
4	Jan	735941	2.12%	18	$ 280,835
5	Feb	694089	2.30%	14	$ 223,497
6	Mar	234919	2.40%	11	$ 62,019
7	Apr	161072	2.40%	20	$ 77,315
8	May	694291	2.40%	15	$ 249,945
9	Jun	493515	2.50%	17	$ 209,744
10	Jul	859359	2.70%	19	$ 440,851
11	Aug	446482	2.70%	18	$ 216,990
12	Sep	754142	2.70%	14	$ 285,066
13	Oct	732016	3.00%	16	$ 351,368
14	Nov	805908	3.00%	20	$ 483,545
15	Dec	810404	3.00%	20	$ 486,242
16	Total				$ 3,367,416

Figure 131

AFTER

	Month	Traffic	Conversion	Average Per uniit	Sales ($)
1			Web		
2					
3	Month	Traffic	Conversion	Average Per uniit	Sales ($)
4	Jan	735941	2.12%	18	$ 280,835
5	Feb	694089	2.30%	14	$ 223,497
6	Mar	234919	2.40%	11	$ 62,019
7	Apr	161072	2.40%	20	$ 77,315
8	May	694291	2.40%	15	$ 249,945
9	Jun	493515	2.50%	17	$ 209,744
10	Jul	859359	2.70%	19	$ 440,851
11	Aug	446482	2.70%	18	$ 216,990
12	Sep	754142	2.70%	14	$ 285,066
13	Oct	732016	3.00%	16	$ 351,368
14	Nov	805908	3.00%	20	$ 483,545
15	Dec	810404	3.00%	20	$ 486,242
16	Total				$ 3,367,416

Figure 132

I just merged the cells in the top row and removed gridlines to clean up the sheet.

If there is a specific style you use – you can save it in your custom format and apply it when needed.

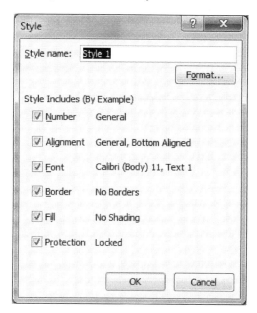

Figure 133

43. Printing

While the world has been talking about paperless office for a while, the fact remains that people still insist on printed copies. This is further true since one of the top uses of Excel is to manage text (lists, etc). However, when many users print they either forget to get grid lines or the column headings. To print an Excel workbook as it appears on a computer screen, follow these steps:

Step 1 – Go to **File, Print, Page Set up**

Figure 134

Step 2 – On the tab **Sheet** select the **Print Area**, **Rows** and **Columns** you want to repeat and if you want Gridlines or not. Three simple selections will greatly enhance your handout quality and usability.

- Print Titles – Rows and Columns to be repeated (for spreadsheets spanning multiple pages)
- Gridlines
- Row and Column headings

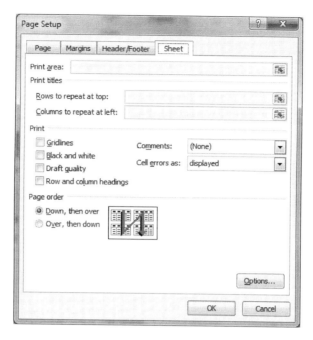

Figure 135

44.   Margins

Sometimes when you are printing a spreadsheet you want everything to fit on one page. Occasionally it is that one extra row that is forcing you to print the additional page and as luck would have it, more often than not that row is the grand total or summary row.

To avoid it you can play around with the margins.

Step 1 – Go to **File, Print, Page Set up**

Step 2 – On the **Margin** tab play around with settings. Also select Center on page and check Horizontally and Vertically.

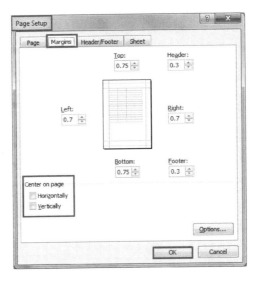

Figure 136

45. Header and Footer

As with any critical document or intellectual property it is a good idea to define a header and footer
. To do so follow these steps:

Step 1 – Go to **File, Print, Page Set up**

Step 2 – Select the **Header/Footer** tab and click on **Custom Header or Custom Footer** to define
what you want to appear. You can input custom text, date, time, workbook name, tab name, etc.

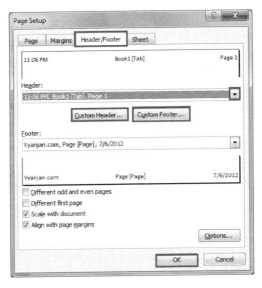

Figure 137

It is one of those little things which starts to add up to make your work look buttoned up.

46. Image as a background of a sheet

Now that we have covered the basics, let us say you really want to jazz up your sheet and you have this amazing picture you want to use as the background to drive home a point. It could be your company's logo or a specific picture such as a fish or sport if your spreadsheet talks about the depleting numbers of fish in local rivers or scores for the little league.

Step 1 – Go to **Page Layout, Background**

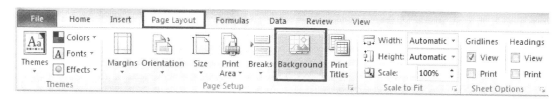

Figure 138

Step 2 – Browse to select the image you want to use as a background and click **Insert**

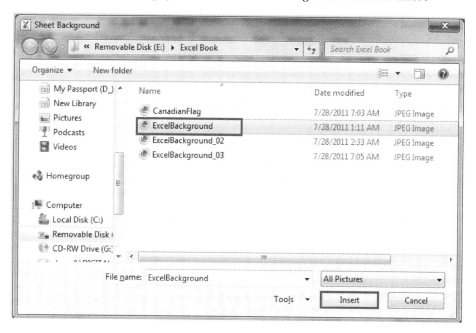

Figure 139

And you are done. The image is the background for the whole spreadsheet.

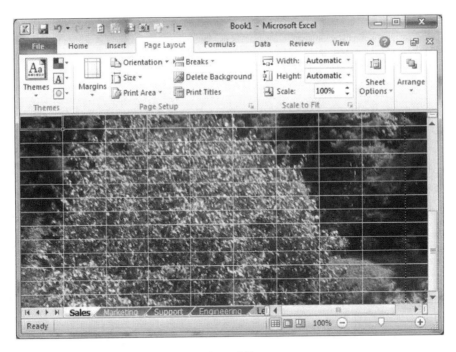

Figure 140

If you want to delete the background – just scroll over to **Page Layout** and click on **Delete background.**

47.   Insert Picture

Sometimes you may want to just add a screenshot into an Excel spreadsheet. For example, if I have the data for the traffic to my book site and I want to add the home page image next to the data, here are the steps.

Step 1 – Launch the page in a browser window or any other application image that you may want to insert.

Step 2 – Move the cursor to where you want to insert the image, in this case cell G11.

	G11	▼	f_x			
	A	B	C	D	E	F	G

	Month	Traffic	Conversion	Average Per un	Sales ($)	
9						
10	**Month**	**Traffic**	**Conversion**	**Average Per un**	**Sales ($)**	
11	Jan	735941	2.12%	18	$ 280,835	
12	Feb	694089	2.30%	14	$ 223,497	
13	Mar	234919	2.40%	11	$ 62,019	
14	Apr	161072	2.40%	20	$ 77,315	
15	May	694291	2.40%	15	$ 249,945	
16	Jun	493515	2.50%	17	$ 209,744	
17	Jul	859359	2.70%	19	$ 440,851	
18	Aug	446482	2.70%	18	$ 216,990	
19	Sep	754142	2.70%	14	$ 285,066	
20	Oct	732016	3.00%	16	$ 351,368	
21	Nov	805908	3.00%	20	$ 483,545	
22	Dec	810404	3.00%	20	$ 486,242	
23	Total				$ 3,367,416	
24						

Figure 141

Step 3 – Go to **Insert, Screenshot**

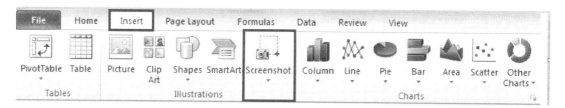

Figure 142

Step 4 – Select the screenshot and resize to adjust it to your needs.

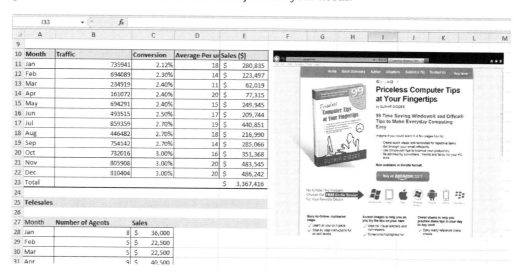

Figure 143

48. Remove Grid lines

If you want a clean look on a coversheet or have a smart art, you might want to remove the Gridlines. To do so go to **View** and uncheck the box **Gridlines**. Your Excel book will appear a lot cleaner and helps your content look more professional!

Figure 144

49. Group and Ungroup

If you have a spreadsheet like the one shown below and you want the monthly data to be hidden but available with a single click you should use **Group.** You can hide the rows but if you want the data to be explicitly known to the user that it exists and can be expanded on demand, then **Group** is the functionality to use.

	Quarter	Month	Traffic	Conversion	Average Per uniit	Sales ($)
8	Web					
9						
10	Quarter	Month	Traffic	Conversion	Average Per uniit	Sales ($)
11	Q1	Jan	735941	2.12%	18	$ 280,835
12	Q1	Feb	694089	2.30%	14	$ 223,497
13	Q1	Mar	234919	2.40%	11	$ 62,019
14		Q1	1664949	2.27%	14	$ 566,350
15	Q2	Apr	161072	2.40%	20	$ 77,315
16	Q2	May	694291	2.40%	15	$ 249,945
17	Q2	Jun	493515	2.50%	17	$ 209,744
18		Q2	1348878	2.43%	17	$ 537,003
19	Q3	Jul	859359	2.70%	19	$ 440,851
20	Q3	Aug	446482	2.70%	18	$ 216,990
21	Q3	Sep	754142	2.70%	14	$ 285,066
22		Q3	2059983	2.70%	17	$ 942,907
23	Q4	Oct	732016	3.00%	16	$ 351,368
24	Q4	Nov	805908	3.00%	20	$ 483,545
25	Q4	Dec	810404	3.00%	20	$ 486,242
26		Q4	2348328	3.00%	19	$ 1,321,155
27	Total					$ 5,413,676

Figure 145

Step 1 - To group the data select the rows, in this case row 11 to 13 and select **Data, Group, Group**

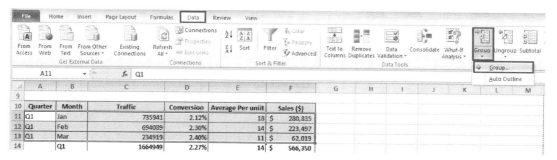

Figure 146

Step 2 - Select **Rows** and Click **OK**

Figure 147

The grouped rows are seen by a small "-"sign.

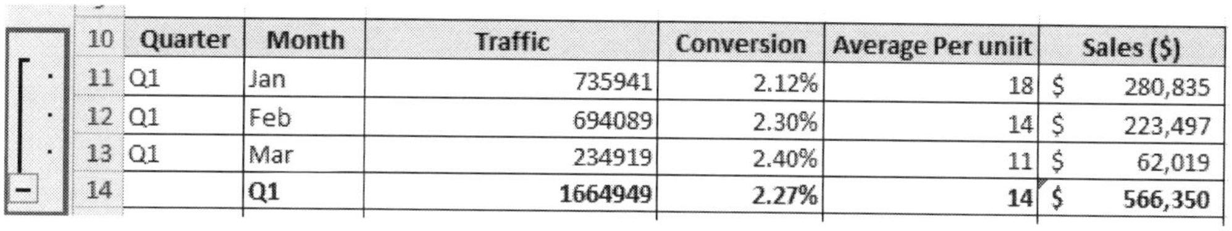

10	Quarter	Month	Traffic	Conversion	Average Per uniit	Sales ($)
11	Q1	Jan	735941	2.12%	18	$ 280,835
12	Q1	Feb	694089	2.30%	14	$ 223,497
13	Q1	Mar	234919	2.40%	11	$ 62,019
14		**Q1**	**1664949**	**2.27%**	**14**	**$ 566,350**

Figure 148

If you group all the quarters and collapse them, the spreadsheet looks like the one shown below. To see the detail a user has to just click on the "+" sign to see the detail.

1 2		A	B	C	D	E	F
	9						
	10	Quarter	Month	Traffic	Conversion	Average Per uniit	Sales ($)
+	14		Q1	1664949	2.27%	14	$ 566,350
+	18		Q2	1348878	2.43%	17	$ 537,003
+	22		Q3	2059983	2.70%	17	$ 942,907
+	26		Q4	2348328	3.00%	19	$ 1,321,155
	27	Total					$ 5,413,676

Figure 149

Grouping is more useful for text and non-numeric aggregation. Sub-total is more effective for numeric aggregation.

50. Subtotal

Subtotal is another useful way to manage data and especially effective in presentation, hence I kept it in the presentation section. Let us again look at the web traffic spreadsheet shown below.

	A	B	C	D	E	F
9						
10	Quarter	Month	Traffic	Conversion	Average Per uniit	Sales ($)
11	Q1	Jan	735941	2.12%	18	$ 280,835
12	Q1	Feb	694089	2.30%	14	$ 223,497
13	Q1	Mar	234919	2.40%	11	$ 62,019
14	Q2	Apr	161072	2.40%	20	$ 77,315
15	Q2	May	694291	2.40%	15	$ 249,945
16	Q2	Jun	493515	2.50%	17	$ 209,744
17	Q3	Jul	859359	2.70%	19	$ 440,851
18	Q3	Aug	446482	2.70%	18	$ 216,990
19	Q3	Sep	754142	2.70%	14	$ 285,066
20	Q4	Oct	732016	3.00%	16	$ 351,368
21	Q4	Nov	805908	3.00%	20	$ 483,545
22	Q4	Dec	810404	3.00%	20	$ 486,242
23	Total					$ 3,367,416

Figure 150

If you wanted subtotals for each quarter, one way would be to manually group and add formulas, another would be to use subtotal command.

Step 1- Select the rows and go to **Data, Subtotal**

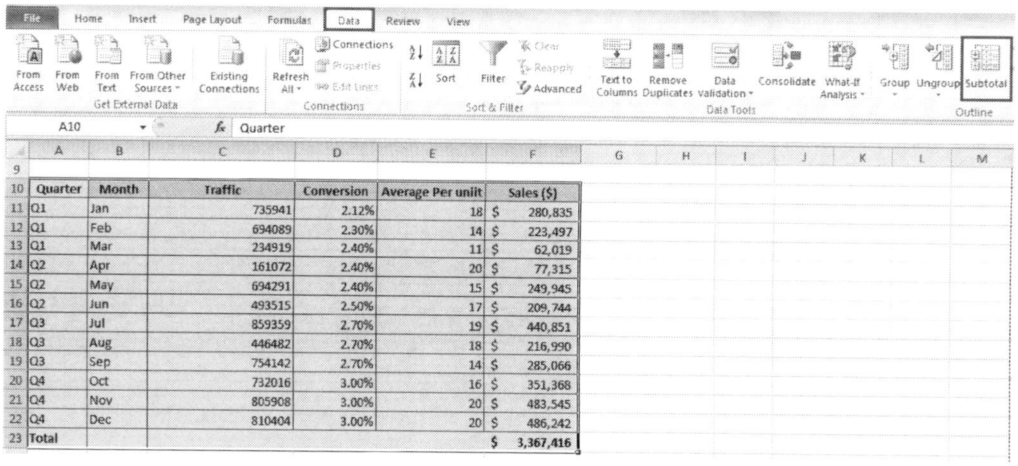

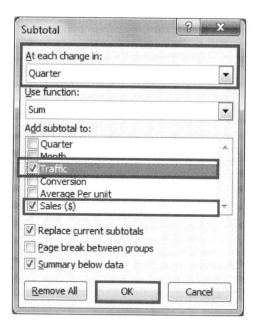

	A	B	C	D	E	F
9						
10	Quarter	Month	Traffic	Conversion	Average Per unit	Sales ($)
11	Q1	Jan	735941	2.12%	18	$ 280,835
12	Q1	Feb	694089	2.30%	14	$ 223,497
13	Q1	Mar	234919	2.40%	11	$ 62,019
14	Q2	Apr	161072	2.40%	20	$ 77,315
15	Q2	May	694291	2.40%	15	$ 249,945
16	Q2	Jun	493515	2.50%	17	$ 209,744
17	Q3	Jul	859359	2.70%	19	$ 440,851
18	Q3	Aug	446482	2.70%	18	$ 216,990
19	Q3	Sep	754142	2.70%	14	$ 285,066
20	Q4	Oct	732016	3.00%	16	$ 351,368
21	Q4	Nov	805908	3.00%	20	$ 483,545
22	Q4	Dec	810404	3.00%	20	$ 486,242
23	Total					$ 3,367,416

Figure 151

Step 2 – Define the Subtotal criteria. In this case we define at each change in Quarter; Add subtotal to Traffic and Sales.

Figure 152

The output appears as shown below with automatic subtotal and outline created for you by Excel.

	Quarter	Month	Traffic	Conversion	Average Per uniit	Sales ($)
11	Q1	Jan	735941	2.12%	18	$ 280,835
12	Q1	Feb	694089	2.30%	14	$ 223,497
13	Q1	Mar	234919	2.40%	11	$ 62,019
14	**Q1 Total**		1664949			$ 566,350
15	Q2	Apr	161072	2.40%	20	$ 77,315
16	Q2	May	694291	2.40%	15	$ 249,945
17	Q2	Jun	493515	2.50%	17	$ 209,744
18	**Q2 Total**		1348878			$ 537,003
19	Q3	Jul	859359	2.70%	19	$ 440,851
20	Q3	Aug	446482	2.70%	18	$ 216,990
21	Q3	Sep	754142	2.70%	14	$ 285,066
22	**Q3 Total**		2059983			$ 942,907
23	Q4	Oct	732016	3.00%	16	$ 351,368
24	Q4	Nov	805908	3.00%	20	$ 483,545
25	Q4	Dec	810404	3.00%	20	$ 486,242
26	**Q4 Total**		2348328			$ 1,321,155
27	**Total**					$ 5,413,676
28	**Total Total**		0			$ 5,413,676
29	**Grand Total**		7422138			$ 8,781,092

Figure 153

Charting

51. Quick Chart

With one keystroke, you can create a new chart or worksheet. To quickly create a chart, select the chart data, and then press **F11**. Let's say you have this data:

	A	B
1	**Month**	**Unit Sales**
2	January	200
3	February	300
4	March	400
5	April	500
6	May	350
7	June	375

Figure 154

To quickly chart it, select the data and just hit **F11**. Here is the default chart that is produced:

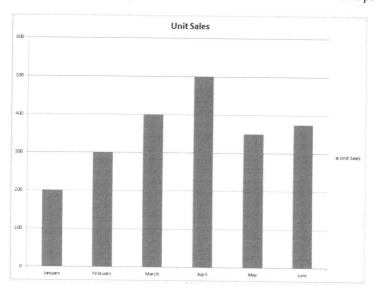

Figure 155

It is produced as its own new worksheet, as "Chart1" in this case. If you don't like it, simply change or delete the chart – your data remains safe.

You can move this chart to either your worksheet or another sheet by selecting the **Move Chart** button in the Excel ribbon:

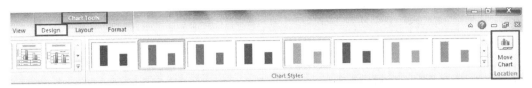

Figure 156

The Move Chart button gives you the option to either place in as a new sheet or as an object in an existing sheet:

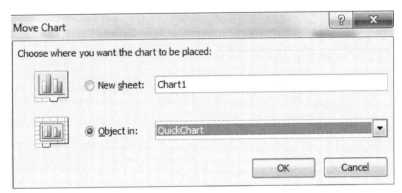

Figure 157

52. Chart Types

More than anything this tip is really to convey the various chart options and how you could use them. The primary purpose of the chart is to help you pack a lot of data that can be consumed visually in a quick amount of time. Nowadays charting has become an art and some of the infographics on the web are truly phenomenal and eye candy for statisticians. However, for the purposes of a normal office user I will list some the charts available in Excel.

- Perhaps the first thing you need to do, is to see what is the relationship between given data variables. Hence a scatter diagram meets your basic needs.
- Second is how does the data compare, say over a time period.
- Third is how is it distributed, like a bell curve or histogram
- Another way to look at it is what the data is composed of; for example, revenue for a company by business units, whether static or trended over time.

Excel provides you the following charts:

Type	Chart use	Basic	Advanced
Relationship	To find the relationship with various data types	Scatter Diagram	Bubble Chart
Comparison		Line Chart	Bubble Chart
Distribution		Histogram Bell curve	Pareto Chart
Composition		Pie chart Column or Bar Chart	Stacked Bar Chart Clustered Column Chart
Trend	Evaluate data trend over a time period Area charts indicate the magnitude of change over time,	Line Chart	Area Chart
Special	Special data relationships chart	Box and Whisker Chart	Surface Chart Donut Chart

One of the best graphics I came across to determine which chart is best suited for a particular data set use is Professor Andrew Abela's chart chooser. Refer to it before making any chart and you will never go wrong.

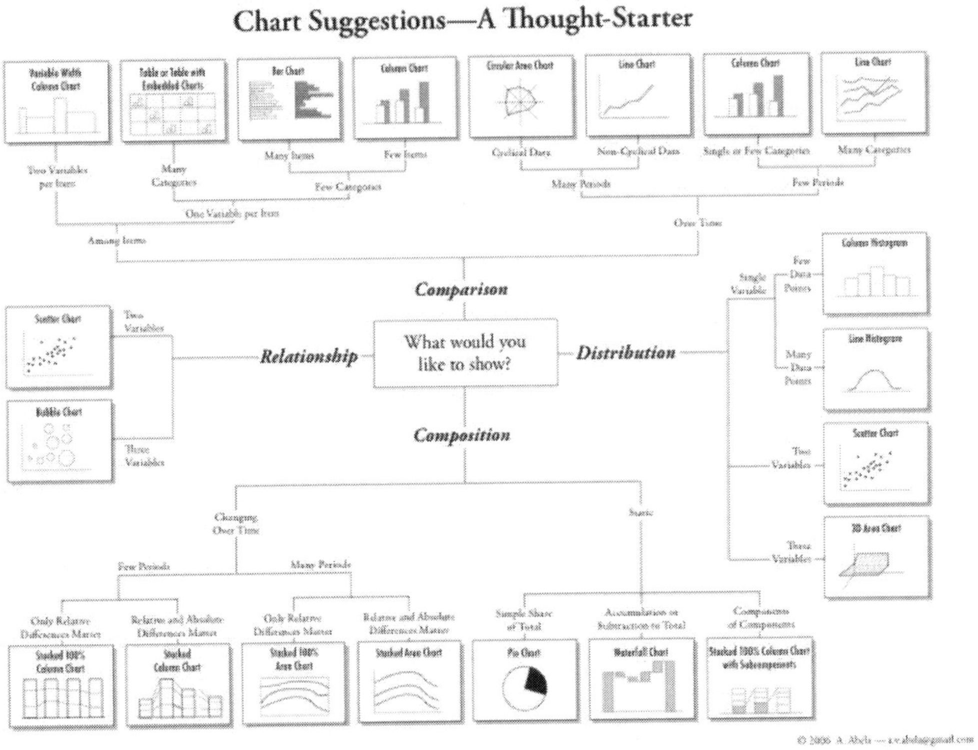

Chart Suggestions—A Thought-Starter

Figure content (flowchart "What would you like to show?" with Comparison, Relationship, Distribution, Composition branches and chart thumbnails):

- Variable Width Column Chart — Two Variables per Item
- Table or Table with Embedded Charts — Many Categories
- Bar Chart — Many Items / Few Items — One Variable per Item
- Column Chart — Few Categories
- Circular Area Chart — Cyclical Data
- Line Chart — Non-Cyclical Data — Many Periods — Over Time
- Column Chart — Single or Few Categories
- Line Chart — Many Categories — Few Periods

Comparison

- Scatter Chart — Two Variables — **Relationship**
- Bubble Chart — Three Variables

What would you like to show?

Distribution
- Single Variable — Few Data Points — Column Histogram
- Many Data Points — Line Histogram
- Two Variables — Scatter Chart
- Three Variables — 3D Area Chart

Composition
- Changing Over Time — Few Periods — Only Relative Differences Matter — Stacked 100% Column Chart
- Relative and Absolute Differences Matter — Stacked Column Chart
- Many Periods — Only Relative Differences Matter — Stacked 100% Area Chart
- Relative and Absolute Differences Matter — Stacked Area Chart
- Static — Simple Share of Total — Pie Chart
- Accumulation or Subtraction to Total — Waterfall Chart
- Components of Components — Stacked 100% Column Chart with Subcomponents

© 2006 A. Abela — a.v.abela@gmail.com

Figure 158

(c) 2012, Andrew V. Abela, Ph.D. www.ExtremePresentation.com<http://www.extremepresentation.com/>
Reproduced with permission.

53. Legend, Axes, Titles

This is not a tip per se, but something you can use to embellish your chart to make it come alive. This will be very useful to non-regular users of Excel who occasionally need to create a chart for developers, designers, engineers, etc.

Once you draw any chart such as a line, column, bar or pie chart, you can make the chart come alive and be much more useful to the readers if you follow the following steps:

Title
- o   Used to define what the chart is all about

Legend
- o   Used to define the various colors used in the chart to represent a series or category

Axes Titles

o   To define the units used in each vertical and horizontal axis

Data Labels

o   Make the data readable as long as there are few values on the chart

Data Table

o   If you want to include the data table on which the chart is based. The rule of thumb is to include a data table as long you have 10-14 cells in the table.

The best way to learn how to use these options is to create a quick chart (Key F11) and try various options under layout as show below. You will soon be creating charts that will be the envy of professional chart makers.

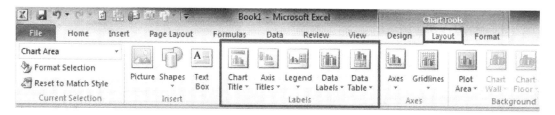

Figure 159

54.   Secondary Axis

This tip is useful if you have to represent two values on a chart, which use different scales. So if you want to show the revenues of a company and number of employees, the scales are different. One might be in thousands of dollars and the other might be in hundreds. We can use a line chart or column chart to represent the data but it is almost impossible to interpret one set of data over the other since the scale is so different. This will become clear in the example below.

Here is the data we are trying to plot.

	A	B	C	D
1	Year	Revenues($ '000s)	Employees	
2	2001	$ 6,000	48	
3	2002	$ 9,000	59	
4	2003	$ 18,000	132	
5	2004	$ 30,000	164	
6	2005	$ 38,000	206	
7	2006	$ 45,000	248	
8	2007	$ 64,000	290	
9	2008	$ 89,000	332	
10	2009	$ 77,000	374	
11	2010	$ 79,000	416	
12	2011	$ 88,000	458	

Figure 160

If we plot it using a standard bar or column chart, the chart looks like this. As you can see below, though the chart is accurate, the bars for number of employees is barely discernible and is dwarfed by the large numbers of the revenue. I have added the data points just to highlight the second chart since it is important to show it exists.

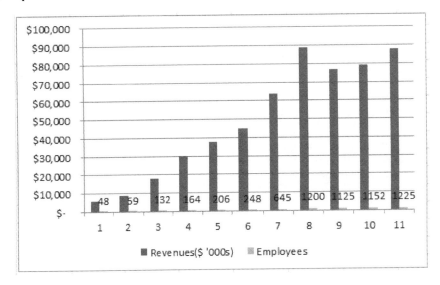

Figure 161

Would it not be cool if each chart had its own axis and we could see both the thousands and hundreds on the same chart?

Fortunately there is an excellent solution in Excel. Here are the steps to accomplish this.

Step 1 – To create a column chart select the data you want to plot and go to **Insert, Column, 2D Clustered Column**

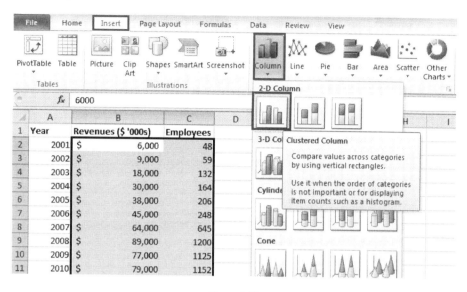

Figure 162

You get the standard chart output. Note there is no Chart Title or Axis Title. Also the years are missing on the Horizontal axis.

Step 2 – To add the years to the horizontal axis select the **Chart** and navigate to **Chart Tools, Design, Select Data**

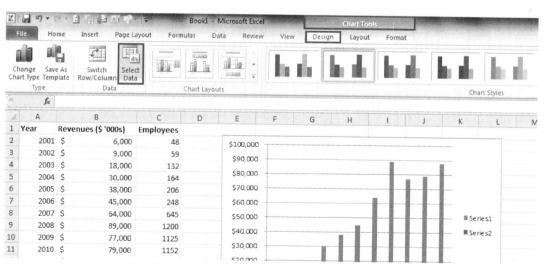

Figure 163

A chart menu will pop up. Click **Edit** as shown below.

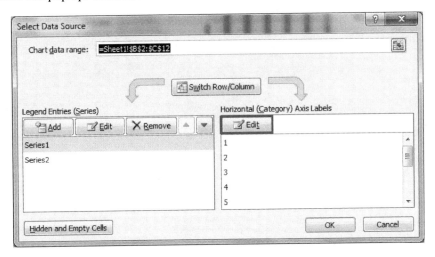

Figure 164

Step 3 – You will see a dialog box like this.

Figure 165

Click Select Range as shown on the box. Just click on cell A2 and while keeping the left mouse button down, drag the mouse to cell A12, and the range will be selected, and click on the box shown.

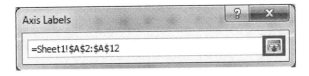

Figure 166

Click **OK**.

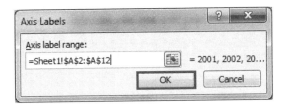

Figure 167

Now you can see the years for the Horizontal (Category) Axis Labels. Click **OK**.

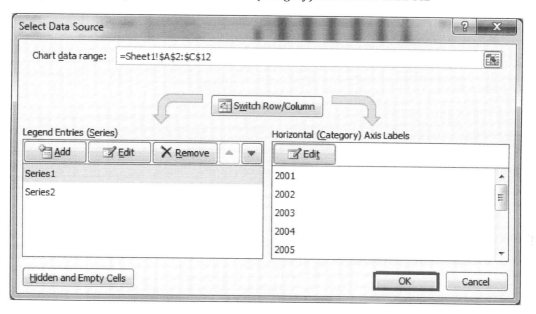

Figure 168

Follow the same steps and select Series1 and Series2 and select the cell B1 and cell C1 for the series names.

Step 3 – Next right click anywhere on the chart data for Series Employees and select Secondary Axis

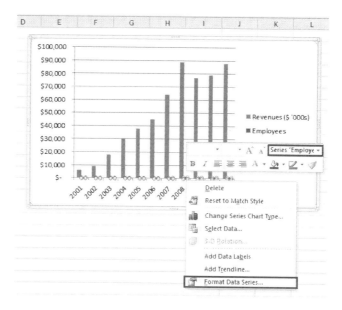

Figure 169

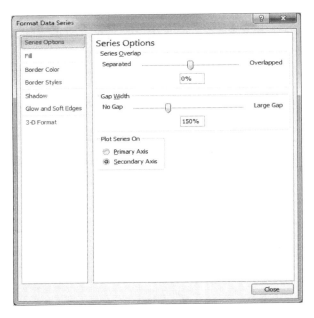

Figure 170

Step 4 – Once you see the chart like the one below, right click on the series Employees and select **Change Chart Type**

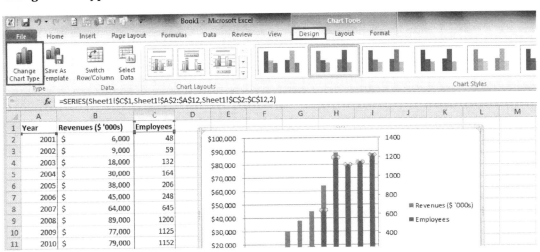

Figure 171

Select **Line** under Change Chart Type

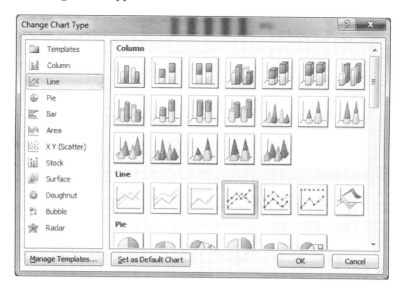

Figure 172

Step 5 - Go and Edit the Chart Title, Primary and Secondary Vertical Axis and legend placement from the options below.

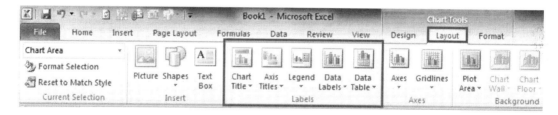

Figure 173

The final chart looks a lot cleaner. The column chart represents revenues which are on the primary or left vertical axis, and the line chart is the number of employees on the secondary or right vertical axis.

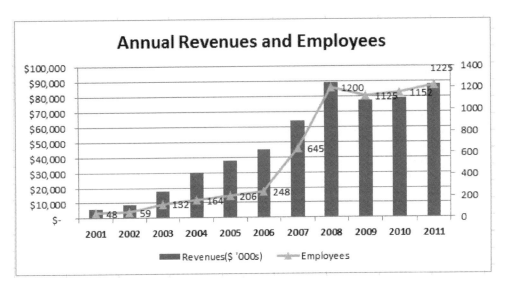

Figure 174

55. Reusable Chart Template

A long time ago I was in a job that required me to create one hundred or so charts - all of which had to be exact with placement of legends and data labels - every month or so. I did that the first time very diligently but after the first time when I was expected to do it all over again the next month I thought there must be a better way. So I ended up writing a macro (a mini program) in Excel that would generate the chart in a second and export it to PowerPoint. I would get through the 100 charts in about an hour. However I would tell my manager it would be a while before I could get through all the charts ☺. The macro served me well as long as I was in the job.

Fortunately now we have Excel Chart Templates. As you can see from the example above – if you have a chart that you need to report often when sticking to a format or layout, you can use Excel Chart Templates.

Here are the steps to follow.

Step 1 – Create a chart with the perfect layout and Axis Titles, Legend Placements, Data Labels, etc. Below is the data and the chart we need to create. You might need to edit the Axis Title, Chart Titles and more, but your chart is effectively ready.

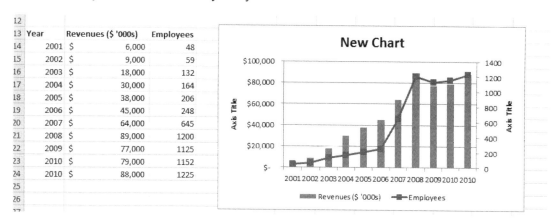

Year	Revenues ($ '000s)	Employees
2001	$ 6,000	48
2002	$ 9,000	59
2003	$ 18,000	132
2004	$ 30,000	164
2005	$ 38,000	206
2006	$ 45,000	248
2007	$ 64,000	645
2008	$ 89,000	1200
2009	$ 77,000	1125
2010	$ 79,000	1152
2010	$ 88,000	1225

Figure 175

Step 2 – Go to Design, Save As Template and Save it as a template with a name. In this case we save the chart as ChartWithSecondaryAxis.

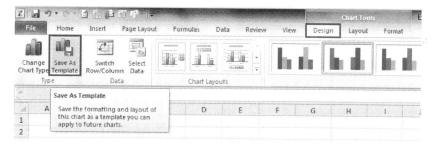

Figure 176

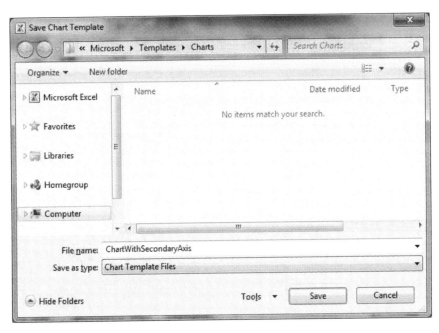

Figure 177

Next time you have the need for a similar chart, select the new template you have defined. In this case we have this new data shown below:

	A	B	C	D	E
1	Year	Revenues ($ '000s)	Employees		
2	1990	$ 600	16		
3	1991	$ 850	19		
4	1992	$ 1,100	20		
5	1993	$ 1,600	27		
6	1994	$ 1,900	36		
7	1995	$ 2,200	45		
8	1996	$ 2,400	64		
9	1997	$ 2,900	81		
10	1998	$ 3,500	100		
11	1999	$ 4,400	121		
12	2000	$ 5,400	144		
13					

Figure 178

Step 3- To create a chart using templates, select the data and go to **Insert, Other Charts, All Charts Types**

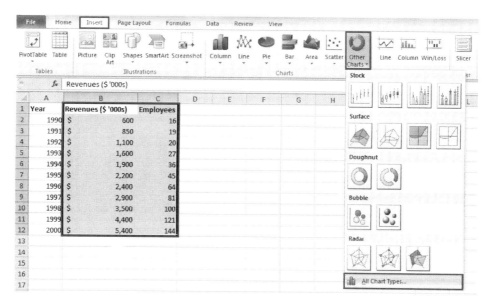

Figure 179

Click **Templates**, **My Templates** and click **OK**

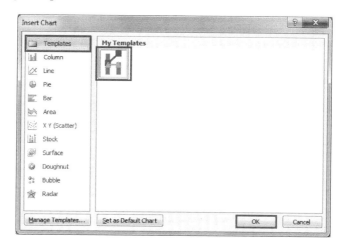

Figure 180

Voila! Your chart is done!

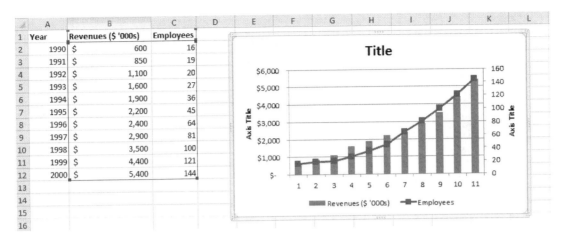

Figure 181

Edit the title and any other edits, and you should be all set.

To delete the chart template from your computer, right-click it, and then click **Delete.**

56. Excel Sparklines

This is so cool. **Excel Sparklines** are a way to visualize data within a single cell, versus using a separate chart. It is very useful when your job involves a lot of data analysis and sharing vast datasets, and is a quick way to summarize data trends by column or by row. Here are the steps to create Sparklines for columns of data:

Step 1 – Enter the data in a row or column. In this case, sales of a book by week.

	A	B	C
1	Book Sales by Week		
2	Week	Sales (Units)	
3	Week 1	5	
4	Week 2	12	
5	Week 3	40	
6	Week 4	75	
7	Week 5	65	
8	Week 6	24	
9	Week 7	82	
10	Week 8	36	
11	Week 9	44	
12	Week 10	28	
13			

Figure 182

Step 2 – Click on **Insert** and select **Column Chart** – not under Charts, but under **Sparklines**

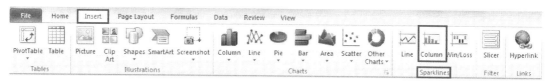

Figure 183

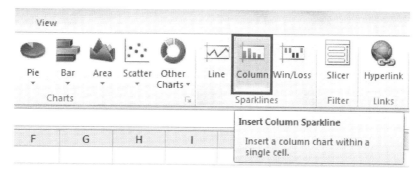

Figure 184

Step 3 – Click on the Column chart and select the data you want included. Also select the destination cell for the chart, which is usually going to be the cell at the end of your data, and click **OK**.

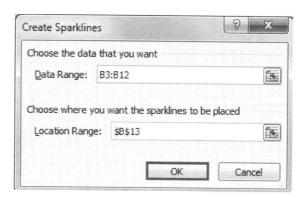

Figure 185

	A	B	C
1	Book Sales by Week		
2	Week	Sales (Units)	
3	Week 1	5	
4	Week 2	12	
5	Week 3	40	
6	Week 4	75	
7	Week 5	65	
8	Week 6	24	
9	Week 7	82	
10	Week 8	36	
11	Week 9	44	
12	Week 10	28	
13			
14			

Figure 186

Step 4 – You will see the column chart in the destination cell B13, as shown below. Imagine how easy it will be to now visually analyze the data for each of several columns.

	A	B	C
1	Book Sales by Week		
2	Week	Sales (Units)	
3	Week 1	5	
4	Week 2	12	
5	Week 3	40	
6	Week 4	75	
7	Week 5	65	
8	Week 6	24	
9	Week 7	82	
10	Week 8	36	
11	Week 9	44	
12	Week 10	28	
13		▁▂▊▊▂▊▆▆▂	
14			

Figure 187

If you want to change the color of the chart, select the cell with the chart, go to the **Design** tab, and select **Sparkline Color.**

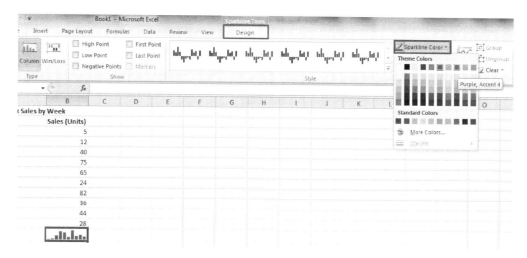

Figure 188

A column chart is good for representing data in a column, such as the above. For data in a row, it may be more useful to use a line chart. Use the steps above, and under Sparklines, choose Line Chart instead of Column Chart. This will give you a trend line representing the data in that row.

57.   Box and Whisker charts

I have been a chart junkie for as long as I can recall. Even before modern graphics became a rage, I used to play with previous versions of spreadsheets and overlay charts to make data more easily consumable. It is in that process I discovered the Box and Whisker chart.

I was in Las Vegas on a holiday and was waiting in line for one of the shows to begin. There was quite a bit of a crowd and two girls who must have been fresh college graduates, who were talking about a recent job interview. One of them said to the other that her last interviewer had asked her about a **Box and Whisker** chart. She said loud enough for me to hear "I have NEVER met anyone who has heard of a Box and Whisker chart. . . the interviewer made it up so that I don't get the job."

I tapped her on the shoulder and said, "I know what it is." It was one of the strangest moments. My intention was to help her, so that if she was ever asked the question in the future, she would know it. I took out a paper napkin and borrowed a pen from someone else in the line and proceeded to quickly explain it to her. She got it instantly, but she did not know the context or why it was called so.

Let us say you have sales data for five years and you want to convey the information in a single chart. Typical interpretation would be to show five line charts or five bar charts and overall the chart may still hide some critical information. This is where the Box and Whisker plot comes in handy. To use this you have to trick Excel a bit.

First thing is to clean the data so that you can show the following for each of the years in exactly this order.

Year	Median	Quartile 1	Maximum	Minimum	Quartile 3

Next plot the data in this order to map to Excel's Volume-Open-High-Low-Close chart. Quartile 1 to Quartile 3 are examples of your open to close values.

Date	Volume	Open	High	Low	Close

If your data looks something like this, then you can plot the chart to show the trend.

Year	Median	Quartile 1	Maximum	Minimum	Quartile 3
Jan-07	200	175	240	150	210
Jan-08	190	172	230	140	205
Jan-09	185	162	225	130	200
Jan-10	160	142	195	120	175
Jan-11	150	132	230	110	180

As you can see, there is an all-up trend which may not be uncovered via normal charts. Pack a lot of information into a small chart to make infographics experts envy your skills.

Here are the steps.

Step 1 – Set up the data as shown above.

Step 2 – Select the data and click **Insert, Other Charts, Stock**. Choose Option 4 **Volume-Open-High-Low-Close**

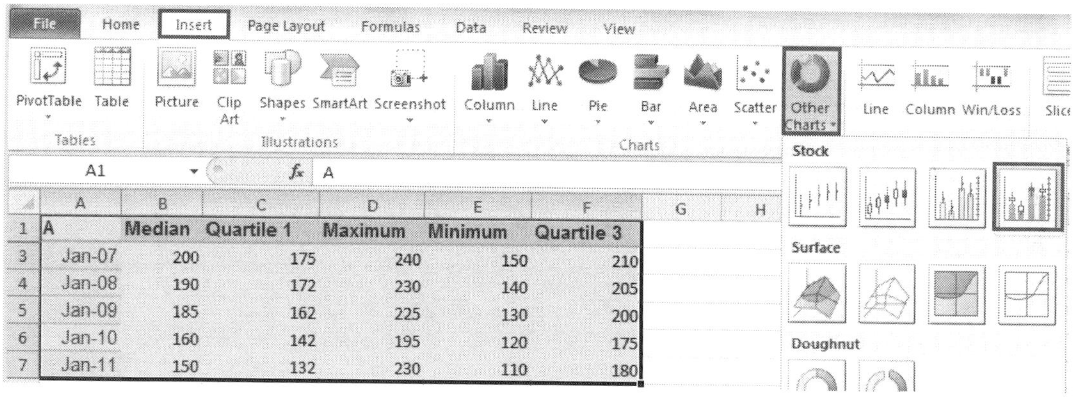

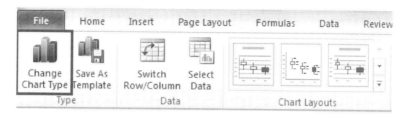

Figure 189

Step 3 – Convert the column chart showing the trend of Median sales by clicking the column chart and changing it to a line chart.

Figure 190

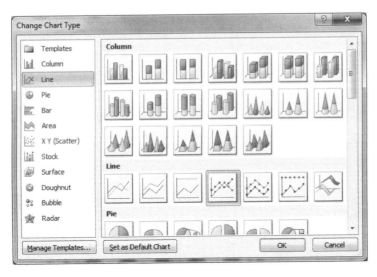

Figure 191

Now go and change the axis to make sure both the primary and secondary axes have the same scale and same point where they cross the X-Axis. The numbers on the primary axis represent the Median Sales. The numbers on the secondary axis represent the Maximum, minimum and the quartiles

Your output looks like this. Note: You can choose the legend, data value and chart title placement as you please.

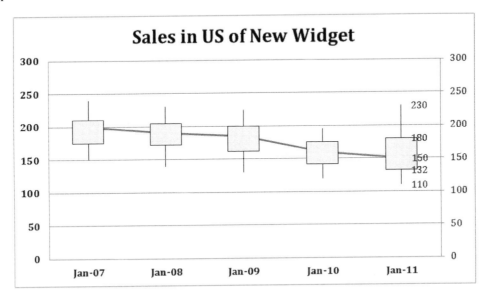

Figure 192

This chart is great for an in-person presentation and not so good for e-mail or non-presentation modes.

58.   Waterfall Chart

This chart is really good for financial analysts or anyone who wants to represent financial data. Let us say you want to show the revenue breakout for a company.

	A	B
1	Annual Sales	Sales $m
2	Books	$ 100
3	Software	$ 45
4	Seminars	$ 21
5	Audio Books	$ 5
6		

Figure 193

To build a waterfall chart follow these steps:

Step 1 – Select the data and go to **Insert, Column, Stacked Column**

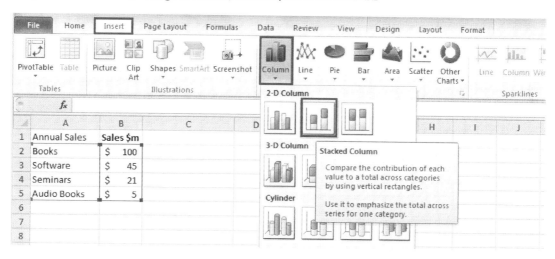

Figure 194

Step 2 – Go to **Design, Layout 9**

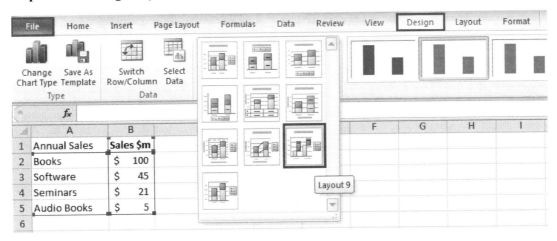

Figure 195

Step 3 – Click on **Switch Row/Column** under Data and you will have the Waterfall chart.

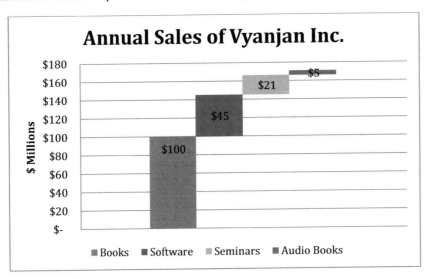

Figure 196

59. Bubble Chart

This is good for product planners and anyone trying to visualize a data set with three variables. Let us say you are in the market to buy a new house and you have selected ten houses and you have a tradeoff to make. To you, the three most important variables in a house are age of the house, square footage, and price. Here is what our data looks like:

	A	B	C
1	Age of the house	Square Footage	Home Price
2	4	2110	$ 505,522
3	17	3600	$ 381,644
4	23	2600	$ 410,629
5	4	2143	$ 482,173
6	10	3090	$ 569,850
7	2	3900	$ 757,039
8	16	3646	$ 543,038
9	7	2668	$ 438,383
10	2	1973	$ 387,478
11	12	2971	$ 375,963
12			

Figure 197

To plot a bubble chart select the data to be plotted and go to Insert, Other Charts, Bubble Chart.

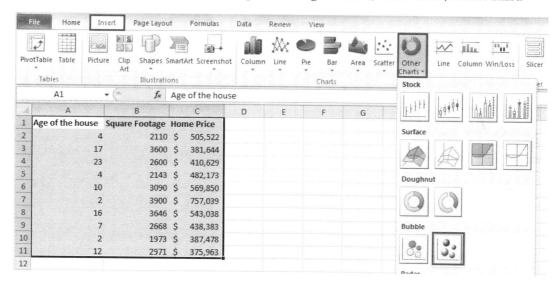

Figure 198

Excel plots the chart for you, which makes it really easy to visually sort the data and make the selection. In this case I cleaned up the Axis Titles and gave the chart a meaningful title.

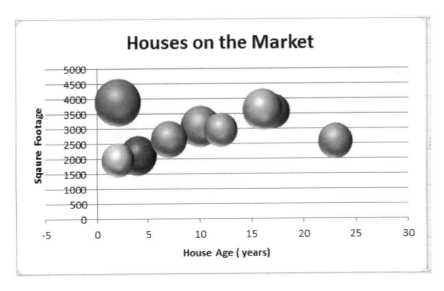

Figure 199

The size of the bubble in the chart is the price of the house, and the other axes are labeled as house age and square footage. Now you can quickly see the bigger and newer house costs. If I want a similar-sized house in a lower budget I should look at houses more than fifteen years old. The more you start to plot data on three variables the more your decision making will improve, especially when you have to make a call on, say, continuing investments in certain products based on revenue growth and installed base.

60.   Change the Marker Symbol

Let us say you have a chart that shows the number of houses sold by month in a city. The data looks like this.

Month	Houses Sold
Jan	123
Feb	89
Mar	92
Apr	143
May	354
Jun	435
Jul	312
Aug	275
Sep	132
Oct	86
Nov	64
Dec	96

If you plot it as a regular line chart it appears like this:

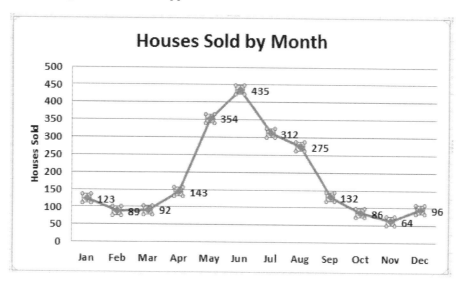

Figure 200

Now, if you were to light up the chart, what if the icons were houses instead of a diamond on the chart. Would the chart not appear a lot cooler?

Step 1 – Click on line in the chart. All the data points are selected as shown in the chart below.

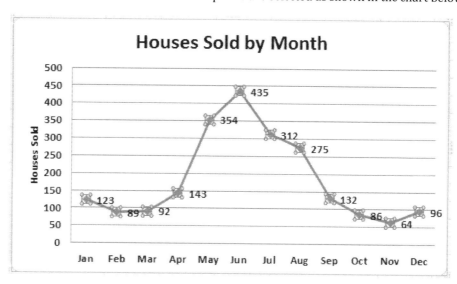

Figure 201

Step 2 – Select the icon you want to use instead of the diamonds. In this case we will use the house from standard Office Clipart gallery. You can use any image.

Figure 202

Step 3 - Click on the new icon and hit **CTRL+C** on your keyboard to copy it.

Step 4 – With the data points selected as in Step 1, click **CTRL+V** on any data point, to paste it. Voila! Your chart suddenly looks a lot better as shown in the chart below. At least you will be able to wow the audience with a professional chart even if the data is less flattering.

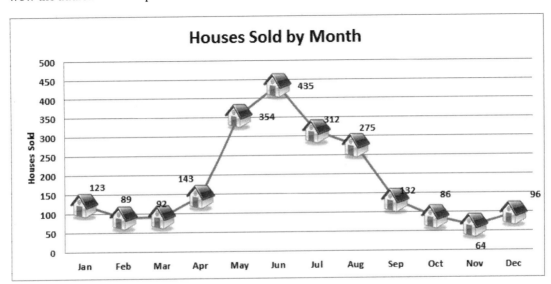

Figure 203

Text Management

61.   Wrap Text

One of the most popular uses of Excel is to manage text in Excel. Don't ask me why, but I have seen more templates and uses of list management in Excel than its actual use for number crunching! No wonder it is one of the world's favorite software programs ever.

As you enter text in Excel, even a long sentence is located within the first cell – no matter how many columns it crosses. But if it exceeds the column width of that first cell, and you have a populated column right next to it, you won't be able to see the rest of that sentence. You can wrap the text so that the words stay visible within that cell. Here is an example before and after wrapping the text. The cell A1 has all of the text.

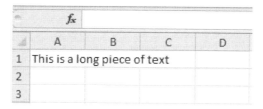

Figure 204

The moment you enter anything in cell B1, the text gets truncated. As you can see, the text in cell A1 is truncated at the fourth word.

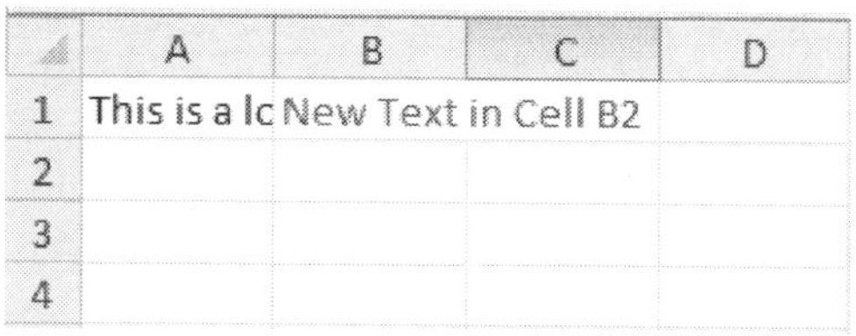

Figure 205

The workaround for this is to go to cell A1 and Select WRAP TEXT as shown below:

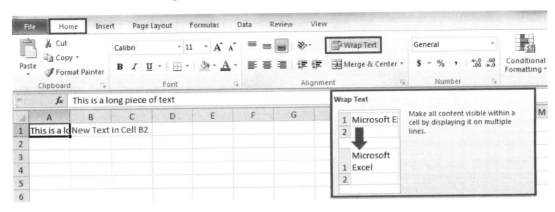

Figure 206

Here is how that looks now: If you want to give it some room, just extend the width of the cell by dragging the line between Columns A and B to the right.

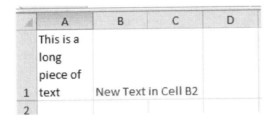

Figure 207

62.   Enter new text row in a cell – ALT+ENTER

To enter a new row in a cell while entering text instead of carriage return just hit **ALT+ENTER**. Below is an example of this.

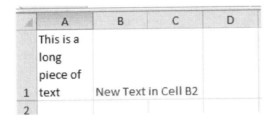

Figure 208

63. Merge and Center

This might be obvious to those of you who know it, but for those who don't, this can make your spreadsheets come alive.

Let us say you are reporting data for sales of a company's product lines by month for a certain year.

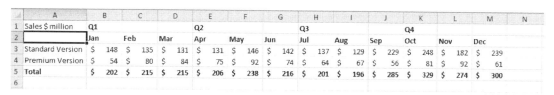

	A	B	C	D	E	F	G	H	I	J	K	L	M	N
1	Sales $ million	Q1			Q2			Q3			Q4			
2		Jan	Feb	Mar	Apr	May	Jun	Jul	Aug	Sep	Oct	Nov	Dec	
3	Standard Version	$ 148	$ 135	$ 131	$ 131	$ 146	$ 142	$ 137	$ 129	$ 229	$ 248	$ 182	$ 239	
4	Premium Version	$ 54	$ 80	$ 84	$ 75	$ 92	$ 74	$ 64	$ 67	$ 56	$ 81	$ 92	$ 61	
5	Total	$ 202	$ 215	$ 215	$ 206	$ 238	$ 216	$ 201	$ 196	$ 285	$ 329	$ 274	$ 300	
6														

Figure 209

Now ideally you could combine cells B, C, and D to show Q1 or Quarter 1. So the steps to achieve this would be:

Step 1 – Select the cells you want to merge, in this case cells B1 to D1.

Step 2 – Go to **Home, Merge & Center**

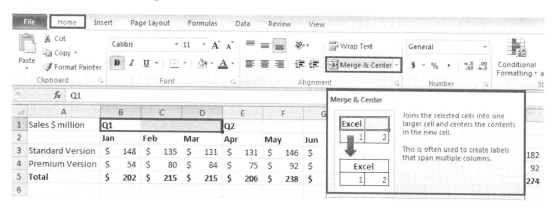

Figure 210

The output looks like this. I have drawn a border around each quarter and added some shading to make the spreadsheet more presentable.

	A	B	C	D	E	F	G	H	I	J	K	L	M	N
1	Sales $ million		Q1			Q2			Q3			Q4		
2		Jan	Feb	Mar	Apr	May	Jun	Jul	Aug	Sep	Oct	Nov	Dec	
3	Standard Version	$ 148	$ 135	$ 131	$ 131	$ 146	$ 142	$ 137	$ 129	$ 229	$ 248	$ 182	$ 239	
4	Premium Version	$ 54	$ 80	$ 84	$ 75	$ 92	$ 74	$ 64	$ 67	$ 56	$ 81	$ 92	$ 61	
5	Total	$ 202	$ 215	$ 215	$ 206	$ 238	$ 216	$ 201	$ 196	$ 285	$ 329	$ 274	$ 300	
6														

Figure 211

64. Alignment

Often you will find cells that need the text to be aligned to the center of a cell. Or in some cases you need the text or content to be aligned to Top/Bottom, for example. To do this, follow these steps.

Step 1 – Expand the Alignment group.

Figure 212

Step 2 – Select from one of the options for Horizontal and Vertical Alignment.

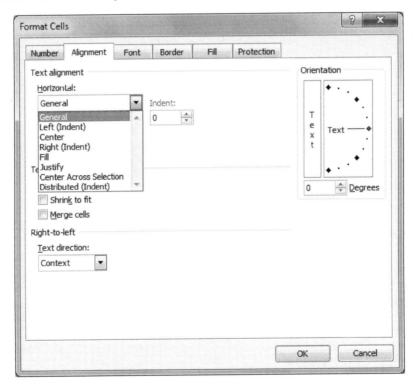

Figure 213

Now often times you have a long column heading but the data in the cells is small so you don't want too wide of columns or the text to wrap either. What do you do?

I will illustrate this. Let us say we have a spreadsheet to track the Olympic gold medals won by countries in various events. We have a spreadsheet which is 200 rows long, to show 200 countries, and 20 possible events across the top, and a column for total. As you can see, the column titles make the column too wide for a medal tally, which is usually a max of two digits, except for the total, which can be three digits.

Figure 214

So to keep the Column heading and yet maintain a clean look, just select the row with the column titles (Row 1) and choose **Home, Angle Counterclockwise** or **Rotate Text Up**.

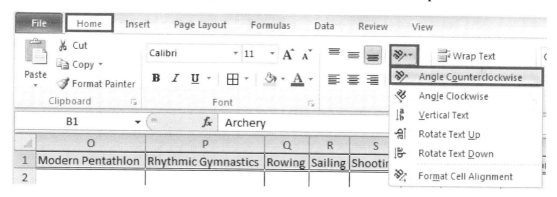

Figure 215

This makes first row wider, but everything else becomes a lot cleaner as you can see below even Synchronized Swimming.

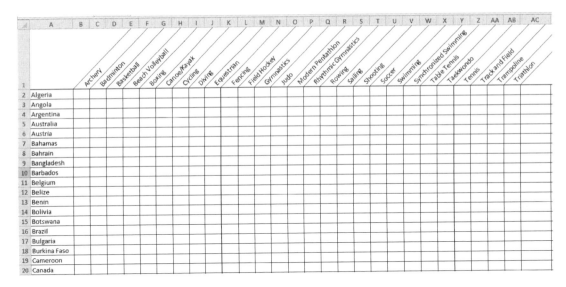

Figure 216

65. Insert a comment in a cell

Given that Excel is used for complex data modeling and tracking of all sorts of things as you build a complex sheet it is a good idea to put comments on a cell to document your assumptions or capture anything special about a data value. For example, if you are projecting the annual sales for a store, you might have data for only six months in one cell instead of the expected 12, because that store opened in July. Or if you are calculating the bonus percentages for a group, you might document Group 1 – 3%, Group 2 – 5%, and Group 3 – 7.5%.

Here are the steps to insert a comment in a cell.

Step 1 – Select the cell you want to insert the comment in, in this case cell A2.

Step 2 – Go to **File, Review, New Comment**

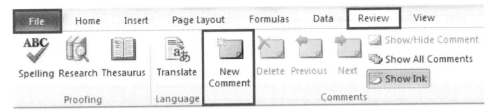

Figure 217

Step 3 – Enter the comment. Each comment is automatically prefixed with your account name on the computer. The presence of the grey margin and dots indicates the comment is in edit mode.

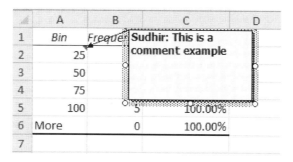

Figure 218

Step 4 – Click anywhere outside that cell and the comment is inserted. Note the presence of a small right triangle on the upper right, indicating the presence of a comment.

Contrary to popular perception, adding a comment does not change the data type of a cell, and hence numerical values remain the same and are not treated as text.

Next time you hover over the cell you will see the comment pop up as shown below.

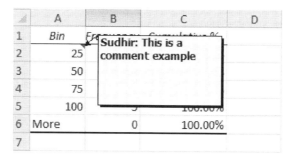

Figure 219

Quick Tip: If you want to insert a comment in a cell just hit **SHIFT+F2** or **ALT+I+M**

66. Show all comments

Let us say as a team you are working on your annual planning sheet and you have a lot of comments in the cells, either it could be to document assumptions on various strategies or different comments by various users.

For example, say you have a spreadsheet that has your marketing plan that captures online marketing, print media, and social media. Now if you want to view all the comments in a spreadsheet just go to **File, Review, Show All Comments.**

Note in the screenshot below I arrange the comments manually to be able to show the comments across cells A2 through A5.

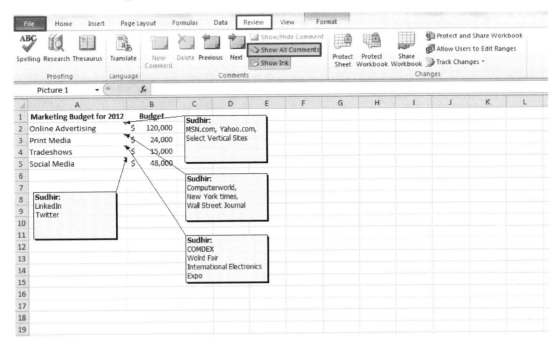

Figure 220

67.   Printing comments of a cell

While some of the experienced users may find the above tip quite basic, not many would know how to print the comments of a cell when printing a worksheet.

Just follow the following steps.

Step 1 – Select the Print Area to print and Go to **File, Print** and choose one of the options.

> Print Active Sheets
> Print Entire Workbook
> Print Selection

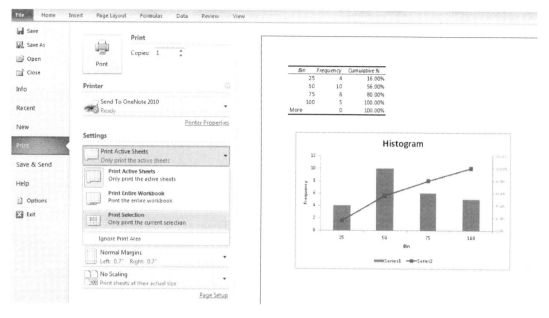

Figure 221

Step 2 – Click on **Page Setup**

Figure 222

Step 3 – Click on **Page Setup, Sheet, Comments**

Step 4 – Make a selection and click **OK**

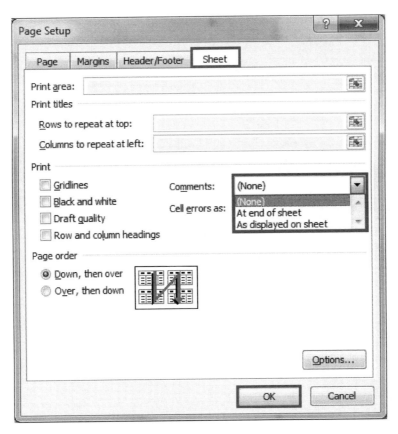

Figure 223

Now when you print, your comments will print, based on your selection.

68. Bullets in Excel

Now this one is a gem. It took me several years to find this out and I am sharing it with you. To create bullets in Excel, here are the steps to create two kinds of bullets:

- To create a solid bullet such as " • ", hit ALT+7
- To create a hollow bullet " ° ", hit ALT+9

Here is an example:

	A	B
1	• For this bullet style use ALT+ 7	
2	o For this bullet style use ALT+ 9	
3		

Figure 224

Note: You have to activate Num Lock (number lock) to use the number 7. On laptops you have to toggle between num lock on and off,otherwise when you type you will start getting numbers instead of characters.

69.   Change Case

Like I mentioned earlier, one of the top uses of Excel is text management. Often you will find when you copy text over into Excel you get all UPPER CASE which makes reading very difficult. Or you have proper case for column headings, and you want to convert this to UPPER CASE. Here is where the text functions come in handy. If you have not read the section on formulas I would refer you to the first couple of tips on formulas to benefit from this and the following tips.

So if you have to convert cell A2 to upper case, in the cell B2 enter the following formula =UPPER(A2). Note that there are no spaces in this formula, and formulas always begin with an = sign.

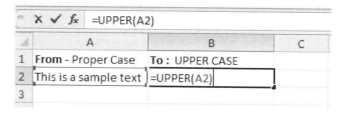

Figure 225

All text is converted to UPPER CASE as in the screenshot below.

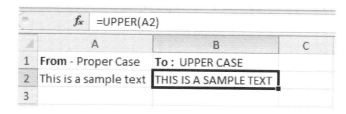

Figure 226

Lower case

To convert a text to lower case, use this formula in any cell: =LOWER(A2) - insert the correct cell.

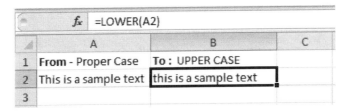

Figure 227

Proper Case

To convert a text to Proper Case where each word has the first letter capitalized, use this formula in any cell =PROPER(A2).

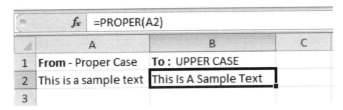

Figure 228

70. Concatenate

Sometimes you have to combine text in two columns or append each column text with a standard text.

Let us say you have two columns with first name and last name.

Normal concatenate:

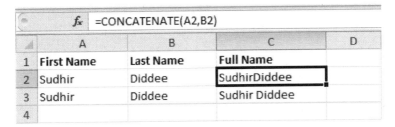

Figure 229

Normal concatenate **with a space** added between the two cells and that starts with creating a space in the formula below

128

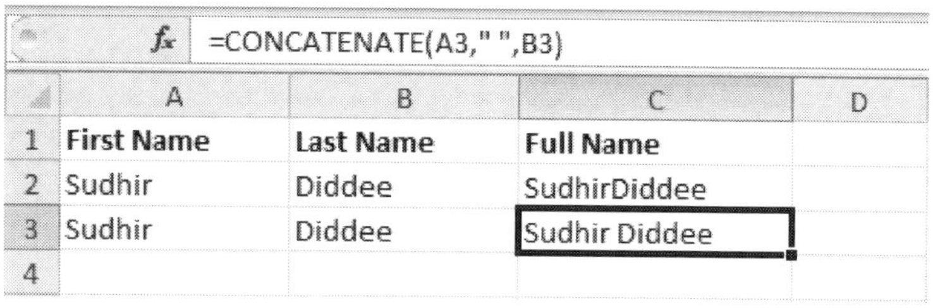

	A	B	C	D
			fx =CONCATENATE(A3," ",B3)	
1	**First Name**	**Last Name**	**Full Name**	
2	Sudhir	Diddee	SudhirDiddee	
3	Sudhir	Diddee	Sudhir Diddee	
4				

Figure 230

Pivot Tables

71. PivotTables

PivotTables are, without a doubt, my favorite feature of Microsoft Excel. Even though they have been around for nearly fifteen years, people may not know about them. Once they know, they love them. But what is the big deal about PivotTables?

Let's say you have some sales data for your company that you want to analyze:

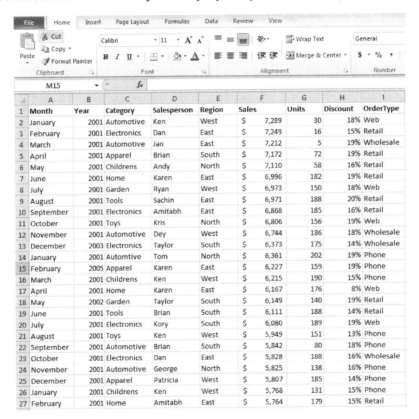

Figure 231

Now let's say you receive three simple questions from your manager:
- Which region had the highest sales by year?
- What are the total sales for each category by region and year?
- Who is your best performing sales person by year?

Normally, it would take you several iterations to come up with the calculations. However, with PivotTables, this is a breeze.

Let's address each question one by one:

Which region had the highest sales by year?

Step 1 - Click on **Insert**, **PivotTable**

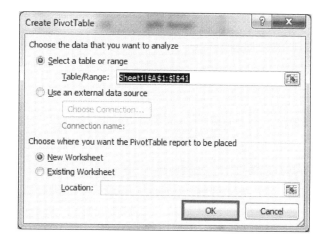

Figure 232

Step 2 - Make the data selection and **Click OK**

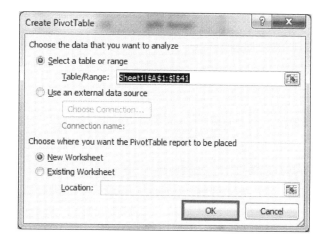

Figure 233

You will see something like this.

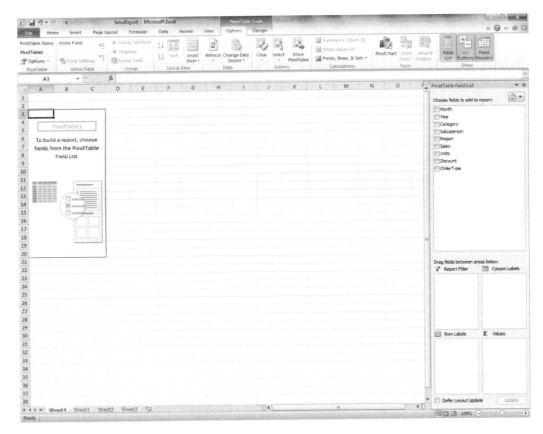

Figure 234

Step 3 - Make your selections by checking and un-checking the boxes and then dragging and dropping the fields in the section Row Labels and Column Labels.

You may ask if we are going to drag and drop the field until we get the answers we are looking for. For the first question, which region had the highest sales by year?

Here is the output:

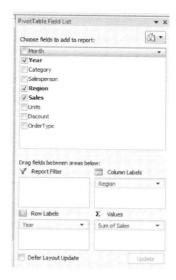

Figure 235

We can quickly see the answer for 2001 and it was the East region which was the highest. And in 2002, it was the South Region.

	A	B	C	D	E	F	G
1							
2							
3	**Sum of Sales**	**Column Labels**					
4	**Row Labels**	**East**	**North**	**South**	**West**	**Grand Total**	
5	2001	$ 58,817	$ 37,192	$ 36,541	$ 44,745	$ 177,295	
6	2002	$ 10,756	$ 10,836	$ 22,163	$ 10,706	$ 54,461	
7	2003			$ 6,373		$ 6,373	
8	2005	$ 6,227				$ 6,227	
9	**Grand Total**	**$ 75,800**	**$ 48,028**	**$ 65,077**	**$ 55,451**	**$ 244,356**	
10							

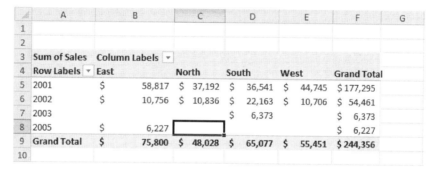

Figure 236

To answer our other questions, we check and uncheck the required fields and get the desired output. Here is a different view of the same data:

3	**Sum of Sales**	**Column Labels**				
4	**Row Labels**	**2001**	**2002**	**2003**	**2005**	**Grand Total**
5	East	$ 58,817	$ 10,756		$6,227	$ 75,800
6	North	$ 37,192	$ 10,836			$ 48,028
7	South	$ 36,541	$ 22,163	$ 6,373		$ 65,077
8	West	$ 44,745	$ 10,706			$ 55,451
9	**Grand Total**	**$ 177,295**	**$ 54,461**	**$ 6,373**	**$6,227**	**$ 244,356**

Figure 237

What are the total sales for each category by region and year?

Figure 238

Here is the output:

3	Sum of Sales	Column Labels					Grand Total
4	Row Labels	2001	2002	2003	2005		Grand Total
5	⊟ East	$ 58,817	$ 10,756		$ 6,227	$	75,800
6	Apparel				$ 6,227	$	6,227
7	Automotive	$ 7,212	$ 5,444			$	12,656
8	Electronics	$ 19,945	$ 5,312			$	25,257
9	Garden	$ 5,762				$	5,762
10	Home	$ 18,927				$	18,927
11	Tools	$ 6,971				$	6,971
12	⊟ North	$ 37,192	$ 10,836			$	48,028
13	Automotive	$ 11,345				$	11,345
14	Automtive	$ 6,361				$	6,361
15	Childrens	$ 7,110				$	7,110
16	Electronics		$ 5,502			$	5,502
17	Garden		$ 5,334			$	5,334
18	Toys	$ 12,376				$	12,376
19	⊟ South	$ 36,541	$ 22,163	$ 6,373		$	65,077
20	Apparel	$ 7,172				$	7,172
21	Automotive	$ 5,842				$	5,842
22	Childrens		$ 5,357			$	5,357
23	Electronics	$ 11,697		$ 6,373		$	18,070
24	Garden		$ 6,149			$	6,149
25	Home		$ 5,345			$	5,345
26	Tools	$ 11,830	$ 5,312			$	17,142
27	⊟ West	$ 44,745	$ 10,706			$	55,451
28	Apparel	$ 5,807	$ 5,410			$	11,217
29	Automotive	$ 14,033				$	14,033
30	Childrens	$ 11,983				$	11,983
31	Garden	$ 6,973				$	6,973
32	Toys	$ 5,949	$ 5,296			$	11,245
33	Grand Total	$ 177,295	$ 54,461	$ 6,373	$ 6,227	$	244,356

Figure 239

Who is your best performing sales person by year? Just move the Sales Person to the Row and Year in the Column and Sales in the Data area to get the answer.

Note, I have included two table level drop-downs. So, if you wanted to see regional reports, you would just click on the drop-down arrows to see, for example, top sales person by year for 2001 and 2002 by region, or by region and category. I also introduced a typo Automotive and Automtive to illustrate the fact that each of them will be treated as a unique value by Excel.

I have just touched the proverbial tip of the iceberg on the power of PivotTables. There are numerous books on PivotTables alone and it is best left to the user to explore all the options. There are literally a hundred books by Microsoft MVPs and other Microsoft Excel experts on the topic if you wish to explore further. Just trust me, you will love PivotTables.

72. Show Values as

If the output of your PivotTable is like the one listed below, you may want to see what percentage of sales were contributed by each category in 2001, 2002 and so on.

Sum of Sales	Column Labels					
Row Labels	2001	2002	2003	2004	2005	Grand Total
Apparel	$ 12,979	$ 5,410			$12,454	$ 30,843
Automotive	$ 38,432	$ 5,444		$ 6,744		$ 50,620
Automtive	$ 6,361			$ 6,361		$ 12,722
Childrens	$ 19,093	$ 5,357		$ 6,215		$ 30,665
Electronics	$ 31,642	$10,814	$ 6,373	$ 9,338	$ 6,373	$ 64,540
Garden	$ 12,735	$11,483		$ 7,405		$ 31,623
Home	$ 18,927	$ 5,345			$ 6,167	$ 30,439
Tools	$ 18,801	$ 5,312		$ 2,976	$ 6,111	$ 33,200
Toys	$ 18,325	$ 5,296	$ 5,225			$ 28,845
Grand Total	$ 177,295	$54,461	$11,598	$39,039	$31,105	$ 313,497

Figure 240

Here are the steps to change how the values are shown in a PivotTable.

Right Click on a field in a PivotTable and scroll to **Show Values As, % of Column Total**

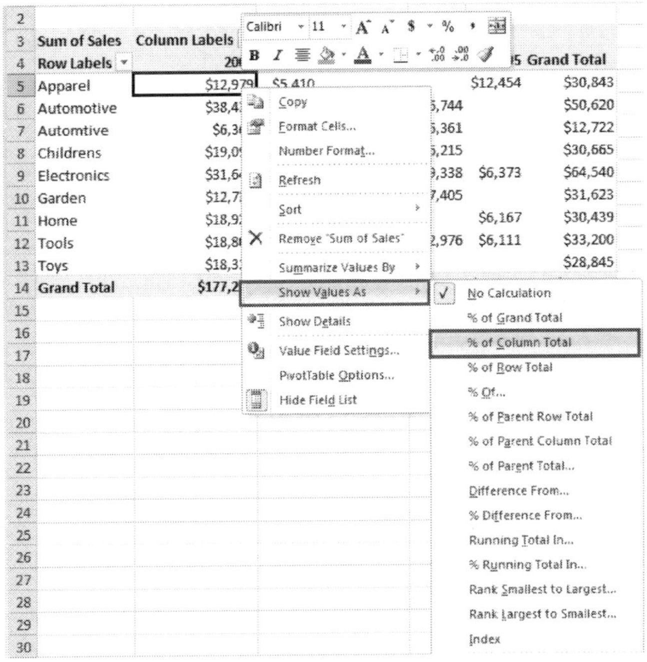

Figure 241

The output changes to:

Sum of Sales	Column Labels					
Row Labels	2001	2002	2003	2004	2005	Grand Total
Apparel	7.32%	9.93%	0.00%	0.00%	40.04%	9.84%
Automotive	21.68%	10.00%	0.00%	17.28%	0.00%	16.15%
Automtive	3.59%	0.00%	0.00%	16.29%	0.00%	4.06%
Childrens	10.77%	9.84%	0.00%	15.92%	0.00%	9.78%
Electronics	17.85%	19.86%	54.95%	23.92%	20.49%	20.59%
Garden	7.18%	21.09%	0.00%	18.97%	0.00%	10.09%
Home	10.68%	9.81%	0.00%	0.00%	19.83%	9.71%
Tools	10.60%	9.75%	0.00%	7.62%	19.65%	10.59%
Toys	10.34%	9.72%	45.05%	0.00%	0.00%	9.20%
Grand Total	100.00%	100.00%	100.00%	100.00%	100.00%	100.00%

Figure 242

It tells us that Automotive contributed to 21.68% of all sales in 2001. All columns are calculated this way. Hence in the Grand Total column shows the total for all the years where Automotive contributed 16.15% of all sales. Note that Excel treats Automotive and Automtive as two different categories. Hence your output is as good as your input.

I would encourage you to play with the options Percentage of Total, Percentage of Row, Running Total, etc. This can be a very useful especially when you are trying various ways to crunch the data to glean new insights.

73. Count, Sum, Average

In a PivotTable by default certain data shows up as sum or count. So if it is a numerical value Excel will automatically return a sum by default. If it is names, since names cannot be added, Excel will show the count of the number of values.

So let us say you have this **PivotTable**

Sum of Sales	Column Labels						
Row Labels	2001	2002	2003	2004	2005	Grand Total	
Apparel	$ 12,979	$ 5,410			$12,454	$ 30,843	
Automotive	$ 38,432	$ 5,444		$ 6,744		$ 50,620	
Automtive	$ 6,361			$ 6,361		$ 12,722	
Childrens	$ 19,093	$ 5,357		$ 6,215		$ 30,665	
Electronics	$ 31,642	$10,814	$ 6,373	$ 9,338	$ 6,373	$ 64,540	
Garden	$ 12,735	$11,483		$ 7,405		$ 31,623	
Home	$ 18,927	$ 5,345			$ 6,167	$ 30,439	
Tools	$ 18,801	$ 5,312		$ 2,976	$ 6,111	$ 33,200	
Toys	$ 18,325	$ 5,296	$ 5,225			$ 28,845	
Grand Total	$ 177,295	$54,461	$11,598	$39,039	$31,105	$ 313,497	

Figure 243

If I want to know how many unique transactions made up Apparel in 2001 and 2002, I would want to see a count by each year for each category.

Select any cell of the PivotTable and Right Click and scroll over to **Summarize Values By, Count.**

Sum of Sales	Column Labels						
Row Labels	$ 2,001	$ 2,002	$ 2,003	$ 2,004	$ 2,005	Grand Total	
Apparel	$ 12,979	$ 5,410			$12,454	$ 30,843	
Automotive	$ 38,432	$ 5,444		$ 6,744		$ 50,620	
Automtive	$ 6,361			$ 6,361		$ 12,722	
Childrens	$ 19,093	$ 5,357		$ 6,215		30,665	
Electronics	$ 31,642	$10,814	$ 6,373	$ 9,338	$ 6,373	64	
Garden	$ 12,735	$11,483		$ 7,405		3:	
Home	$ 18,927	$ 5,345			$ 6,167	$ 30,439	
Tools	$ 18,801	$ 5,312		$ 2,976	$ 6,111	3:	
Toys	$ 18,325	$ 5,296	$ 5,225			28	
Grand Total	$ 177,295	$54,461	$ 11,598	$39,039	$31,105	$ 313	

Calibri 11 A A $ %
B I ≡ A

- Copy
- Format Cells...
- Number Format...
- Refresh
- Sort
- × Remove "Sum of Sales"
- Summarize Values By → ✓ Sum
- Show Values As → Count
- Show Details — Average
- Value Field Settings... — Max
- PivotTable Options... — Min
- Show Field List — Product
- More Options...

Figure 244

Once you do that also change the format of the cells to Number or General. Now we know Automotive has six transactions in 2001 and one each in 2002 and 2004.

	A	B	C	D	E	F	G
1	Region	(All)					
2							
3	Count of Sales	Column Labels					
4	Row Labels		2001	2002	2003	2004	2005 Grand Total
5	Apparel		2	1			2
6	Automotive		6	1		1	8
7	Automtive		1			1	2
8	Childrens		3	1		1	5
9	Electronics		5	2	1	2	1
10	Garden		2	2		2	6
11	Home		3	1			1
12	Tools		3	1		1	1
13	Toys		3	1	1		5
14	Grand Total		28	10	2	8	5
15							

Figure 245

You can change the values to average, maximum, minimum, etc.

You can also change how the PivotTable summarizes the data by right-clicking on the field list of the PivotTable and click to change the value field settings.

Figure 246

Step 2 - Click on **Value Field Settings**

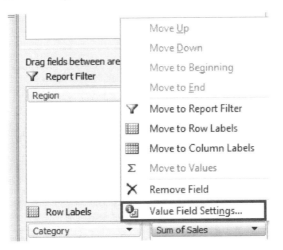

Figure 247

Step 3 – Change the options under **Summarize value field by** and click **OK**

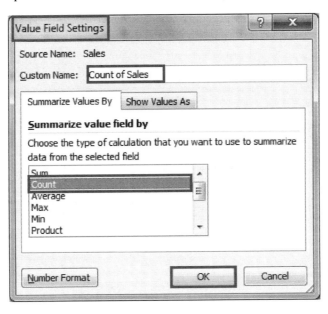

Figure 248

74. Format

Similar to the presentation of an Excel spreadsheet, a little bit of work on a PivotTable presentation will make a world of difference to put a bow around the great analysis you might have done.

You can either do some minor cosmetic changes or really soup up the PivotTable by applying Table Styles to an Excel PivotTable.

The PivotTable has a default formatting applied to it. If you want to change minor formatting then you can go to the design view and make changes to the default layout by selecting such things as sub-totals and banded rows to change the views.

Let us say you have the PivotTable view as shown below:

	A	B	C	D	E	F	G
1							
2							
3	OrderType	(All)					
4	Units	(All)					
5	Sales	(All)					
6	Salesperson	(All)					
7							
8	Sum of Sales	Region					
9	Year	East	North	South	West	Grand Total	
10	2001	$ 58,817	$ 37,192	$ 36,541	$ 44,745	$ 177,295	
11	2002	$ 10,756	$ 10,836	$ 22,163	$ 10,706	$ 54,461	
12	2003			$ 6,373	$ 5,225	$ 11,598	
13	2004		$ 9,619	$ 13,485	$ 15,935	$ 39,039	
14	2005	$ 18,621		$ 12,484		$ 31,105	
15	Grand Total	$ 88,194	$ 57,647	$ 91,046	$ 76,610	$ 313,497	
16							

Figure 249

To change the look and feel and to make it more readable we can change the columns to be banded or alternately shaded. Click anywhere on the PivotTable and Go to **Design**, **Banded Columns**

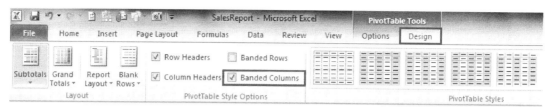

Figure 250

The PivotTable changes to the following view. You also get the options of showing Subtotals and Grand Totals, and choose the option that makes most sense for your report and its readability.

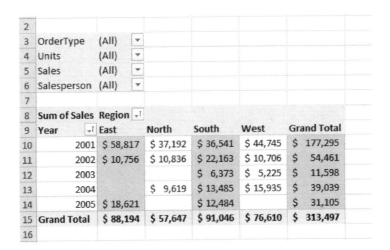

Sum of Sales	Region				
Year	East	North	South	West	Grand Total
2001	$ 58,817	$ 37,192	$ 36,541	$ 44,745	$ 177,295
2002	$ 10,756	$ 10,836	$ 22,163	$ 10,706	$ 54,461
2003			$ 6,373	$ 5,225	$ 11,598
2004		$ 9,619	$ 13,485	$ 15,935	$ 39,039
2005	$ 18,621		$ 12,484		$ 31,105
Grand Total	$ 88,194	$ 57,647	$ 91,046	$ 76,610	$ 313,497

Figure 251

Now if you want to change the look and feel significantly, you can use PivotTable Styles. Click on the Pivot Table and select one of the Style options.

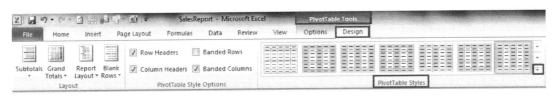

Figure 252

If you click on the down arrow on the extreme right you will be presented with a whole set of options for the PivotTable look and feel.

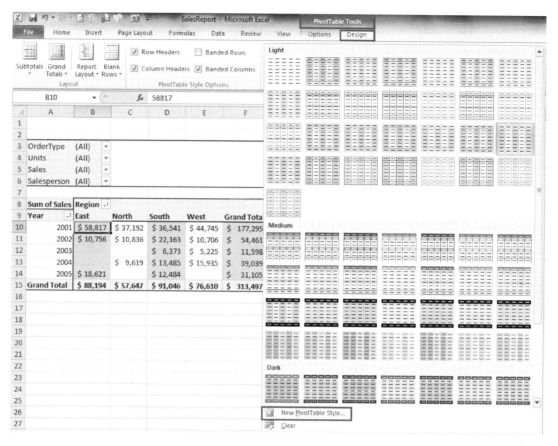

Figure 253

If none of these options meet your needs then select the New PivotTable Style and you will be
presented with a pop-up screen where you can define your custom style.

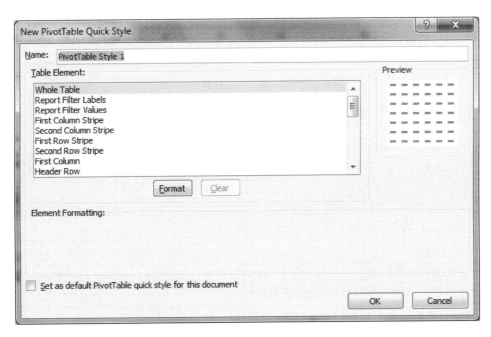

Figure 254

You can customize the style and select the checkbox "Set as the Default PivotTable quick style for this document" and name it. Then your custom style is available to you every time you want to apply it for other PivotTables in that document.

75. Slicers

As you might have noticed you can filter the PivotTable based on a set of values. You can select region from the drop down and filter the PivotTable only on East region. One drawback of this is that a user may forget what the filter is set on, or that one has been applied at all, and may use the data without resetting the filters or adding other filters for his or her needs.

Slicers are in essence graphical filters. They tell you visually what filters are on or off. So in the PivotTable below, if I add the Slicer this is what it looks like.

The steps to add the slicer are:

Step 1 - Click anywhere in the PivotTable and go to **Options, Insert Slicers, Insert Slicer**

Figure 255

Step 2 – Select Region in the pop-up window. You can select multiple slicers in the PivotTable.

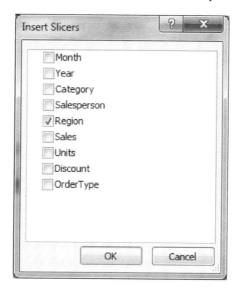

Figure 256

Step 3 – The slicer appears in the Excel spreadsheet. You can move the window to where you would like it to be placed on the spreadsheet -- move the window while holding the left click.

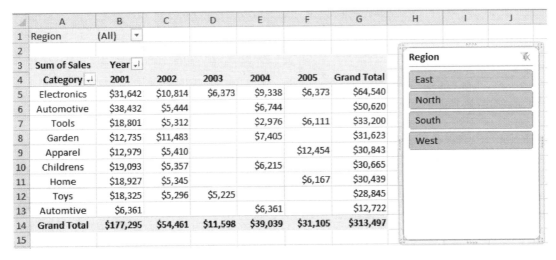

Figure 257

Here is an example with multiple Slicers. I have filtered on East Region and Year 2001, and selected a different color for each filter.

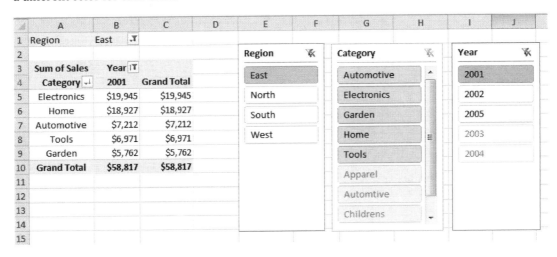

Figure 258

To remove a slicer, just highlight the slicer window and hit delete. The view is reset and the underlying data is not deleted.

76. Drill Down on PivotTable

Here is a real life story. One day I came into work and was reviewing the reports with one of my coworkers for sales by district of various products we were managing. I looked at the data and found my colleague had missed an important variable, which meant he had to create all the reports with the new variable added in. I casually remarked, "Why don't you edit and update these reports with the correct data and let us reconvene in half an hour?"

My colleague looked at me with rage in his eyes and finally he blurted it out. "Do you even know how long it took me to put together these reports?"

"No, but it should not have been more than ten minutes at most."

"I spent the whole of yesterday getting these views together for you." He was almost out of breath as he blurted those words out.

"Did you use the PivotTable Drill-Down option?" I asked.

He said he had no idea what it was. I went over to his desk and proceeded to show him the details for each of the districts in a single click and he was both REALLY MAD and really appreciative. Long story short, he committed himself to mastering PivotTables and in a short time with a little bit of help, he became a rock star and the go-to person on the team on Excel PivotTables.

Let me show you how this works. I will use a simple example, but this is extremely powerful if you use it on a complex PivotTable.

Here is the PivotTable for our base data.

Region	(All)					
Sum of Sales	**Year**					
Category	**2001**	**2002**	**2003**	**2004**	**2005**	**Grand Total**
Electronics	$31,642	$10,814	$6,373	$9,338	$6,373	$64,540
Automotive	$38,432	$5,444		$6,744		$50,620
Tools	$18,801	$5,312		$2,976	$6,111	$33,200
Garden	$12,735	$11,483		$7,405		$31,623
Apparel	$12,979	$5,410			$12,454	$30,843
Childrens	$19,093	$5,357		$6,215		$30,665
Home	$18,927	$5,345			$6,167	$30,439
Toys	$18,325	$5,296	$5,225			$28,845
Automtive	$6,361			$6,361		$12,722
Grand Total	**$177,295**	**$54,461**	**$11,598**	**$39,039**	**$31,105**	**$313,497**

Figure 259

Now if I want to see the data for West region I can just select West in the Region and I can get the summary view of West region as below.

	A	B	C	D	E	F
1	Region	West				
2						
3	**Sum of Sales**	**Year**				
4	**Category**	**2001**	**2002**	**2003**	**2004**	**Grand Total**
5	Automotive	$14,033			$6,744	$20,777
6	Childrens	$11,983			$6,215	$18,198
7	Toys	$5,949	$5,296	$5,225		$16,469
8	Apparel	$5,807	$5,410			$11,217
9	Garden	$6,973				$6,973
10	Tools				$2,976	$2,976
11	**Grand Total**	**$44,745**	**$10,706**	**$5,225**	**$15,935**	**$76,610**

Figure 260

But what if the person in charge of the Western region wanted to see the details of the entire data? One way might be to go to the raw data and filter each of the settings to get the report. It might be easy for data that is relatively simple but if you had to do the same for a fairly complex set of reports for a number of sales regions/countries, your reaction might be similar to my colleague's.

One way to get the details is to right-click on any cell and get the details. In this case I click on cell F11 that shows a value of $76,610 and right-click to **Show Details**.

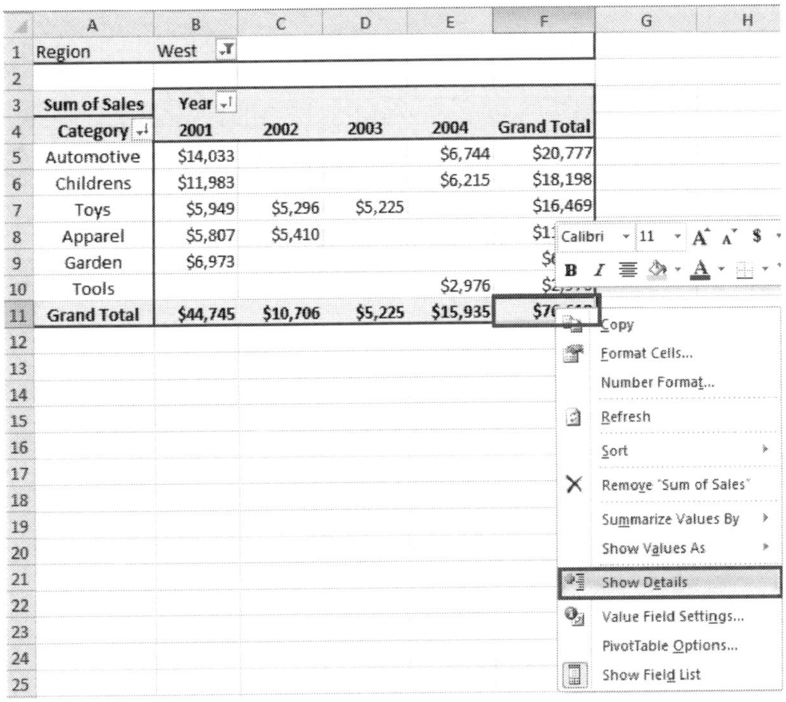

Figure 261

The output is shown below. Note this is only for the West region.

	A	B	C	D	E	F	G	H	I
1	Month	Year	Category	Salesperson	Region	Sales	Units	Discount	OrderType
2	December	2001	Apparel	Patricia	West	5807	185	13.7%	Phone
3	October	2002	Apparel	Patricia	West	5410	155	13.1%	Wholesale
4	January	2001	Automotive	Ken	West	7289	30	18.2%	Web
5	Novembe	2001	Automotive	Dey	West	6744	186	17.6%	Wholesale
6	Novembe	2004	Automotive	Jon	West	6744	186	17.6%	Wholesale
7	January	2001	Childrens	Ken	West	5768	131	14.7%	Phone
8	March	2001	Childrens	Ken	West	6215	190	15.1%	Phone
9	March	2004	Childrens	Ken	West	6215	190	15.1%	Phone
10	July	2001	Garden	Ryan	West	6973	150	17.5%	Web
11	January	2004	Tools	Scott	West	2976	59	6.0%	Retail
12	August	2001	Toys	Ken	West	5949	151	13.1%	Phone
13	April	2002	Toys	Karen	West	5295.5	154	13.7%	Wholesale
14	May	2003	Toys	Robert	West	5224.924	96	9.0%	Retail

Figure 262

If I had right clicked on cell B7 I would have gotten the output as shown below:

	A	B	C	D	E	F	G	H	I
1	Month	Year	Category	Salesperson	Region	Sales	Units	Discount	OrderType
2	August	2001	Toys	Ken	West	5949	151	13.1%	Phone

Figure 263

As you can see it shows the details of the data that makes up that cell for the given set of PivotTable options.

77. Pivot Chart

Apart from the fact that PivotTables are excellent tools to crunch data, very few people use the PivotCharts options. This allows you to dynamically visualize the data and see which visualization best supports the argument you are putting forth.

We will use the same data source to calculate a PivotChart. Here are the steps.

Step 1 - To create a pivot chart, select any cell within the PivotTable you created and navigate to **Options, Pivot Chart**

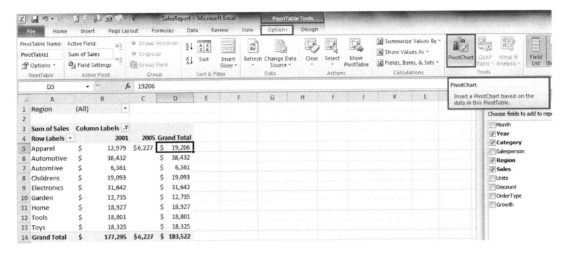

Figure 264

Step 2 - Select the **Chart Type**. In this example we will use the Column and click **OK**

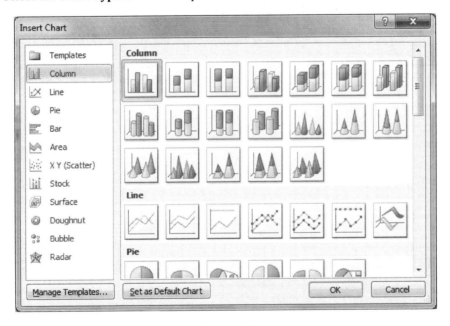

Figure 265

The output will be a chart as follows:

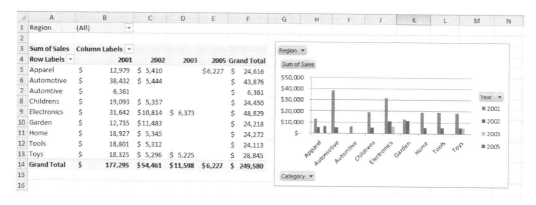

Figure 266

Now you can change the visualization by filtering directly on the chart. So if I want to view East, I can go to the Region drop down **on the chart** and filter on East region.

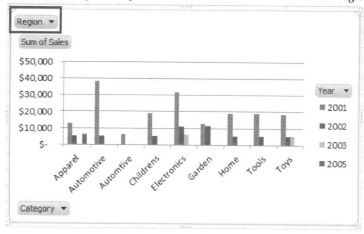

Figure 267

Figure 268

The chart output is shown below. The filter icon on the chart implies a filter has been applied to the data.

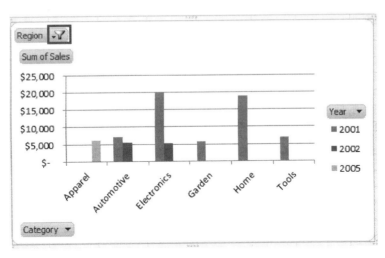

Figure 269

You can drag the year to the X axis and Category to the Y axis to dynamically list and change the chart view in the PivotTable field list. In this case I swapped the row and column.

Figure 270

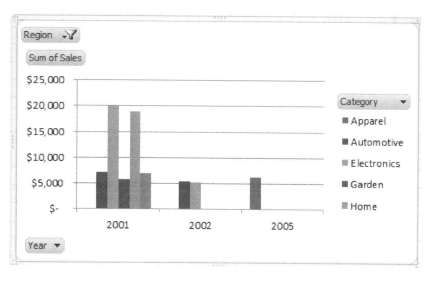

Figure 271

You should try other options, like changing the chart type or changing the values to averages to see how the chart changes.

78. Calculated Field

Let us say you have sales data (partial view) as shown and the associated PivotTable (partial view)

	A	B	C	D	E	F	G	H	I
1	Month	Year	Category	Salesperson	Region	Sales		Units	Discount	OrderType
2	January	2001	Automotive	Ken	West	$	7,289	30	18%	Web
3	February	2001	Electronics	Dan	East	$	7,249	16	15%	Retail
4	March	2001	Automotive	Jan	East	$	7,212	5	19%	Wholesale
5	April	2001	Apparel	Brian	South	$	7,172	72	19%	Retail
6	May	2001	Childrens	Andy	North	$	7,110	58	16%	Retail
7	June	2001	Home	Karen	East	$	6,996	182	19%	Retail
8	July	2001	Garden	Ryan	West	$	6,973	150	18%	Web
9	August	2001	Tools	Sachin	East	$	6,971	188	20%	Retail
10	September	2001	Electronics	Amitabh	East	$	6,868	185	16%	Retail
11	October	2001	Toys	Kris	North	$	6,806	156	19%	Web
12	November	2001	Automotive	Dey	West	$	6,744	186	18%	Wholesale
13	December	2003	Electronics	Taylor	South	$	6,373	175	14%	Wholesale
14	January	2001	Automtive	Tom	North	$	6,361	202	19%	Phone
15	February	2005	Apparel	Karen	East	$	6,227	159	19%	Phone
16	March	2001	Childrens	Ken	West	$	6,215	190	15%	Phone

Figure 272

◢	A	B	C	D
1	Region	(All) ▼		
2	OrderType	(All) ▼		
3	Year	(All) ▼		
4				
5		**Values**		
6	**Salesperson** ▼	**Sum of Sales**	**Sum of Units**	
7	Ken	$31,436	692	
8	Dan	$18,839	363	
9	Jan	$7,212	5	
11	Allie	$6,373	175	
12	Amitabh	$12,632	364	
13	Andy	$12,612	195	
14	Ankur	$6,361	202	
15	Brian	$24,742	477	
16	Dey	$6,744	186	
17	Gabriel	$6,080	189	
18	George	$5,825	138	

Figure 273

What if you had a very simple query – what is the sales per unit by sales person? The simple way would be to put the formula in column D and be done with it. But as soon as you change the view by dragging and dropping the fields of the PivotTable, the formula will be over-written and you will lose the values. Ideally you would like to see it integrated as a part of the PivotTable.

Well there is an option called **Calculated Field.** A user can define a field that is a calculation as a part of the PivotTable and once the field is created it can be dragged, dropped and manipulated like any other field of the PivotTable.

In our example we want to define **Sales per Unit = Sales/Units**.

To create a **Calculated Field** follow these steps:

Step 1: Click anywhere inside the PivotTable and go to **Options, Field, Items and Sets, Calculated Field**

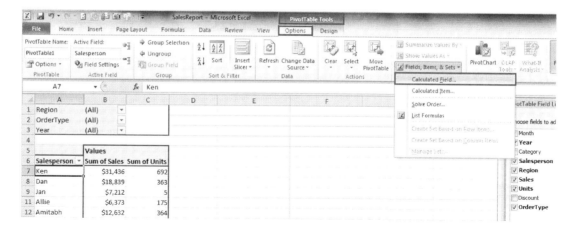

Figure 274

Step 2: Enter the **Name** of the field and **Enter the formula**. In this case I select Sales and click on **Insert Field** and enter the "/ " sign and again select Units and click **Insert Field** again.

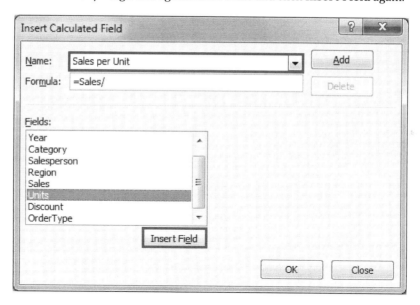

Figure 275

Step 3: Click **Add, OK** to exit the pop-up window.

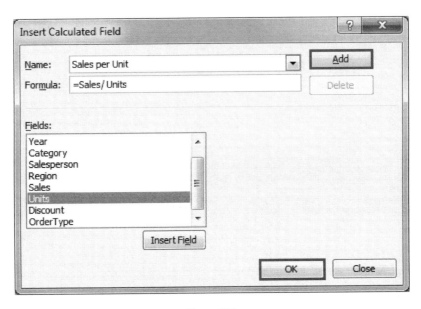

Figure 276

We instantly get the new field as a part of the PivotTable. Note the field is not formatted as a currency field, since the PivotTable does not know any better.

	A	B	C	D	E
1	Region	(All)			
2	OrderType	(All)			
3	Year	(All)			
4					
5		Values			
6	Salesperson	Sum of Sales	Sum of Units	Sum of Sales per Unit	
7	Ken	$31,436	692	45.42774566	
8	Dan	$18,839	363	51.89807163	
9	Jan	$7,212	5	1442.4	
11	Allie	$6,373	175	36.41714286	
12	Amitabh	$12,632	364	34.7032967	
13	Andy	$12,612	195	64.67692308	
14	Ankur	$6,361	202	31.49009901	
15	Brian	$24,742	477	51.87002096	
16	Dey	$6,744	186	36.25806452	
17	Gabriel	$6,080	189	32.16931217	

Figure 277

You can go and edit the field. Click anywhere in the PivotTable and Field list is displayed on the right. Left click on the new Calculated Field and select **Value Field Settings**.

156

Figure 278

Select Number Format

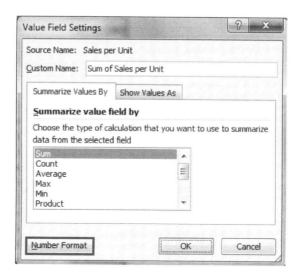

Figure 279

Choose **Currency** and Click **OK**

Figure 280

The output is shown as follows:

	A	B	C	D	E
1	Region	(All) ▾			
2	OrderType	(All) ▾			
3	Year	(All) ▾			
4					
5		Values			
6	Salesperson ▾	Sum of Sales	Sum of Units	Sum of Sales per Unit	
7	Ken	$31,436	692	$45.43	
8	Dan	$18,839	363	$51.90	
9	Jan	$7,212	5	$1,442.40	
11	Allie	$6,373	175	$36.42	
12	Amitabh	$12,632	364	$34.70	
13	Andy	$12,612	195	$64.68	
14	Ankur	$6,361	202	$31.49	
15	Brian	$24,742	477	$51.87	
16	Dey	$6,744	186	$36.26	
17	Gabriel	$6,080	189	$32.17	
18	George	$5,825	138	$42.21	
19	Glen	$6,227	159	$39.16	

Figure 281

There you have a new calculated field in the PivotTable. You can enter any combination of formulas as a new field to suit your needs.

79. Calculated Item

Calculated Item is a very useful feature of the PivotTable. Think of it as a new aggregation row or column. In the following PivotTable, if I wanted to view a set of sales persons as a unit every time because they belonged to a certain category such as managers, or they were formerly in the Central region, I can create a new row called Manager or Central to see how they are performing as a unit. Let me illustrate it with the following example.

In the following PivotTable, if I want to group Patricia, Brian, Dan, Andy, Ken, and Karen into one group called **Central,** follow the steps outlined below.

	A	B	C	D	E
1	OrderType	(All)			
2	Year	(All)			
3	Region	(All)			
4					
5		Values			
6	Salesperson	Sum of Sales	Sum of Units	Sum of Sales per Unit	
7	Ken	$31,436	692	$45.43	
8	Dan	$18,839	363	$51.90	
9	Jan	$7,212	5	$1,442.40	
11	Allie	$6,373	175	$36.42	
12	Amitabh	$12,632	364	$34.70	
13	Andy	$12,612	195	$64.68	
14	Ankur	$6,361	202	$31.49	
15	Brian	$24,742	477	$51.87	
16	Dey	$6,744	186	$36.26	
17	Gabriel	$6,080	189	$32.17	
18	George	$5,825	138	$42.21	
19	Glen	$6,227	159	$39.16	
20	Janet	$5,719	159	$35.97	
21	Jon	$6,744	186	$36.26	
22	Joy	$6,149	140	$43.92	
23	Karen	$24,686	671	$36.79	
24	Kory	$11,437	335	$34.14	
25	Kris	$6,806	156	$43.63	
26	Mark	$3,258	79	$41.24	
27	Mason	$6,111	188	$32.51	
28	Patricia	$11,217	340	$32.99	
29	Robert	$5,225	96	$54.43	
30	Ryan	$6,973	150	$46.49	
31	Sachin	$17,727	470	$37.72	
32	Samir	$6,167	176	$35.04	
33	Sanjay	$1,256	39	$32.21	
34	Scott	$2,976	59	$50.44	
35	Taylor	$23,437	616	$38.05	
36	Tom	$17,215	483	$35.64	
37	Grand Total	$313,497	7631	$41.08	

Figure 282

Step 1: Click anywhere in the row where you want the new **Calculated Item.** Go to **Options, Calculated Item**

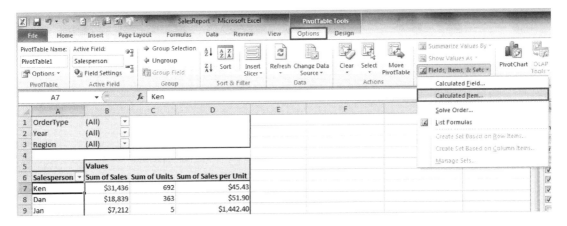

Figure 283

Step 2: Enter the new formula for the Calculated Item, in this case I am calling it Central and the formula is Central = Patricia+Brian+Dan+Andy+Ken+Karen.

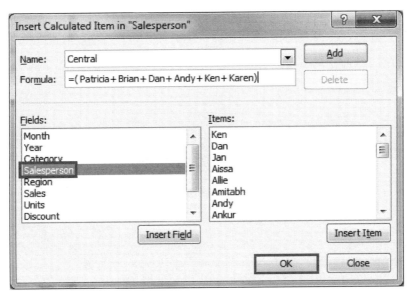

Figure 284

Now you can see I have the last row as the new Calculated Item called Central. Note I have hidden new rows of the PivotTable to make the table appear smaller for the purpose of the screenshot below.

	A	B	C	D	E
1	OrderType	(All) ▾			
2	Year	(All) ▾			
3	Region	(All) ▾			
4					
5		Values			
6	Salesperson ▾	Sum of Sales	Sum of Units	Sum of Sales per Unit	
25	Kris	$6,806	156	$43.63	
26	Mark	$3,258	79	$41.24	
27	Mason	$6,111	188	$32.51	
28	Patricia	$11,217	340	$32.99	
29	Robert	$5,225	96	$54.43	
30	Ryan	$6,973	150	$46.49	
31	Sachin	$17,727	470	$37.72	
32	Samir	$6,167	176	$35.04	
33	Sanjay	$1,256	39	$32.21	
34	Scott	$2,976	59	$50.44	
35	Taylor	$23,437	616	$38.05	
36	Tom	$17,215	483	$35.64	
37	Central	$123,532	2738	$45.12	
38	Grand Total	$437,029	10369	$42.15	

Figure 285

80.   Add a Rank to the PivotTable

Sometimes when you are analyzing data you are limited by the column and row heading. So in the case of our PivotTable we can sort by the salesperson or region or category. What if we ranked all the sales?

Click in the PivotTable field area, right click **Show Values As, Rank Smallest to Largest**

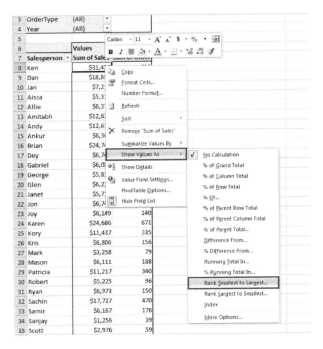

Figure 286

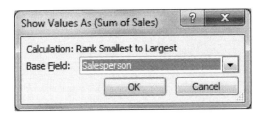

Figure 287

Now the PivotTable shows the sales in order by rank, showing in our case that Sanjay has the least and Ken has the most sales. If you ranked largest to smallest, the ranking would show Ken as 1 and Sanjay as 29. You can add back the sales to see the sales calculation.

	A	B	C	D
1				
2				
3	OrderType	(All)		
4	Year	(All)		
5				
6		Values		
7	Salesperson	Sum of Sales	Sum of Units	
8	Ken	29	692	
9	Dan	25	363	
10	Jan	18	5	
11	Aissa	5	143	
12	Allie	14	175	
13	Amitabh	22	364	
14	Andy	21	195	
15	Ankur	13	202	
16	Brian	28	477	
17	Dey	15	186	
18	Gabriel	8	189	
19	George	7	138	
20	Glen	12	159	
21	Janet	6	159	
22	Jon	15	186	
23	Joy	10	140	
24	Karen	27	671	
25	Kory	20	335	
26	Kris	16	156	
27	Mark	3	79	
28	Mason	9	188	
29	Patricia	19	340	
30	Robert	4	96	
31	Ryan	17	150	
32	Sachin	24	470	
33	Samir	11	176	
34	Sanjay	1	39	
35	Scott	2	59	
36	Taylor	26	616	
37	Tom	23	483	
38	Grand Total		7631	

Figure 288

The new view might look like this if ranked largest to smallest. I cleaned, formatted, and took a slice of the PivotTable to show what the data might look like for ease of understanding.

	Salesperson	Sum of Sales	Sum of Sales2	Sum of Units
1				
2	OrderType	(All)		
3	Year	(All)		
4	Region	(All)		
5				
6		Values		
7	Salesperson	Sum of Sales	Sum of Sales2	Sum of Units
8	Ken	1	$ 31,436	692
9	Brian	2	$ 24,742	477
10	Karen	3	$ 24,686	671
11	Taylor	4	$ 23,437	616
12	Dan	5	$ 18,839	363
13	Sachin	6	$ 17,727	470
14	Tom	7	$ 17,215	483
15	Amitabh	8	$ 12,632	364
16	Andy	9	$ 12,612	195
17	Kory	10	$ 11,437	335
18	Patricia	11	$ 11,217	340

Figure 289

Advanced Power Tips

81.   Copy Cell contents from the cell above

If you have a cell you want copied to the next row, then type CTRL+ '(apostrophe) or CTRL+D. The cell is copied immediately. Note you can achieve the same by dragging the anchor or CTRL+C and CTRL+V but once you start using the combination of CTRL+' you will notice the change in efficiency, particularly if you have to repeat it more than a few times a day.

82.   Move a selection in Excel

To move a selection quickly in Excel, select the cells and move the cursor to the appropriate edge in the direction you want to move. The cursor changes to a **CROSSHAIR**. Now while holding down the **LEFT CLICK** drag the selection to its new destination.

In the example below I am moving the cells to D6.

Figure 290

And, voila!

Figure 291

83.   Quick Formatting Shortcuts

Here are some of my favorite quick formatting shortcuts, which are hard to discover but very useful in day-to-day use.

Key	Description
CTRL+SHIFT+& (ampersand)	Applies border to the selected cells
CTRL+SHIFT+_ (underscore)	Removes the outline border from selected cells
CTRL+SHIFT+!	Applies number format with two decimal places, thousands separator and minus sign for negative values
CTRL+SHIFT+*	Selects current region around the active cell
ALT+=	Automatically adds all the cells in the selection

84.   Change Gridline Color

There are some tricks which just make you appear cool. Changing Gridline color is one of them. For the longest time I had not imagined changing Gridline color to anything other than black. Then I discovered it in Excel 2007 and it is carried over in Excel 2010. How you will use this is up to you, but if you do change it – the first question you will get asked is "How did you do it?" This is one of those tips that Excel junkies love.

To change Gridline color, follow these steps.

Go to **File, Options, Advanced** – scroll to the **Display options** for this worksheet and select the Grid line color. In this example I chose "Green" and clicked OK.

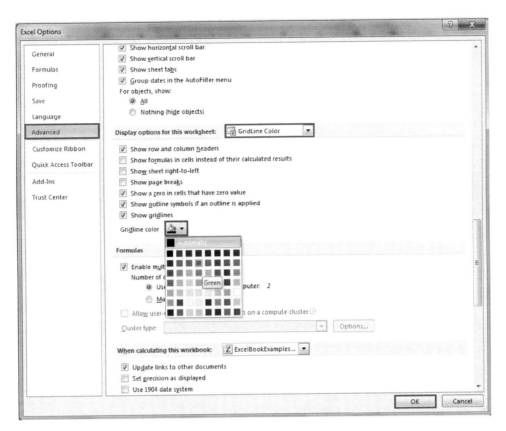

Figure 292

I recommend trying it with a color like pink, red, or brown to see the impact.

85. Change the position of Quick Access Toolbar

The Quick Access toolbar is to quickly get to commands you use very often. Normally it appears above the Excel workbook ribbon. To show it below the workbook, check the box next to Show Quick Access Toolbar below the Ribbon.

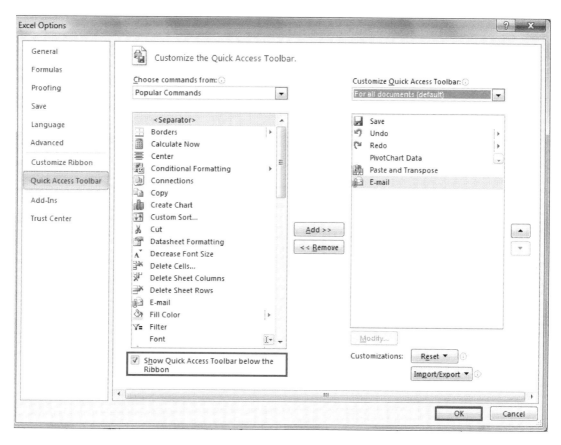

Figure 293

Click OK and you are done.

The Quick Access Toolbar now appears below the ribbon.

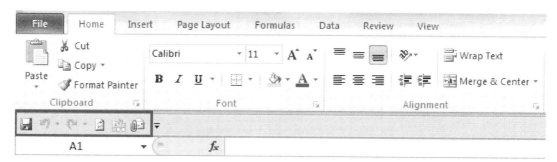

Figure 294

86.   Change the shape of a comment

One way to enhance the spreadsheet is to edit the shape of the comment. In the above example it would be cool to have different comment shapes for each spend category.

For example, in a spreadsheet that has your marketing plan that captures online marketing, print media, social media, etc., you can use a different shape for each comment. This is another tip that will have people asking you, "how did you DO that?"

Let us say for online we choose the comment shape as a cloud, for print it's a rectangle, for trade shows it is a cylinder, and so on.

Here are the steps to change the Onlline comment from a rectangle to a bubble.

Step 1 – Move the cursor to the cell with the comment and display the comment. Go to File, Review, and Show/Hide Comment.

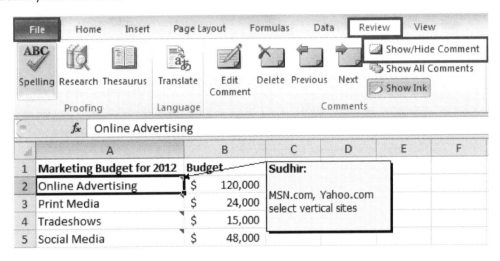

Figure 295

Step 2 – Go to **Quick Access Toolbar** and select **More Commands** from the drop down.

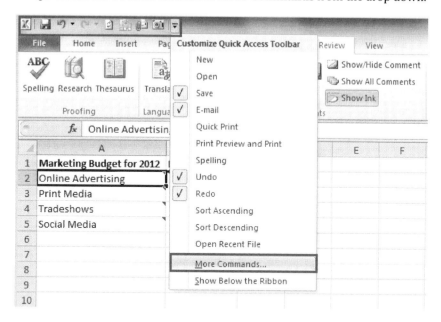

Figure 296

Step 3 – Select **All Commands**, Select **Change Shape** and click **Add, then** click **OK**

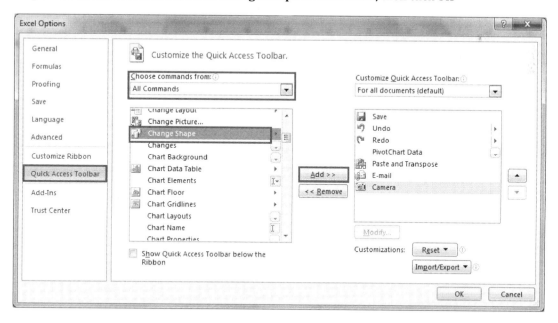

Figure 297

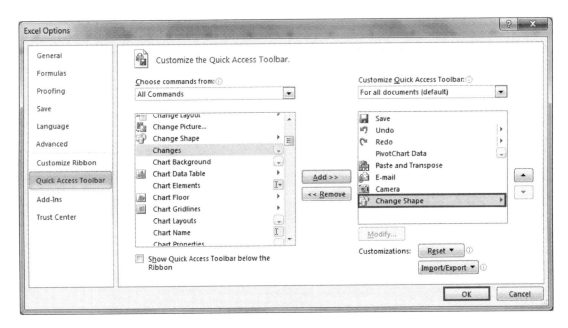

Figure 298

Step 4 – Note the new **Change Shape** icon in the Quick Access Toolbar.

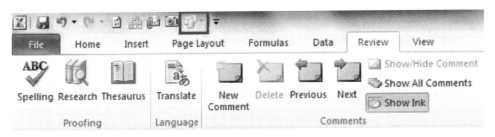

Figure 299

Step 5 – Select the Comment you want to edit, in this case cell A2, and while the comment is active click on the Change Shape icon on the Quick Access Toolbar and select the new shape, in this case the cloud.

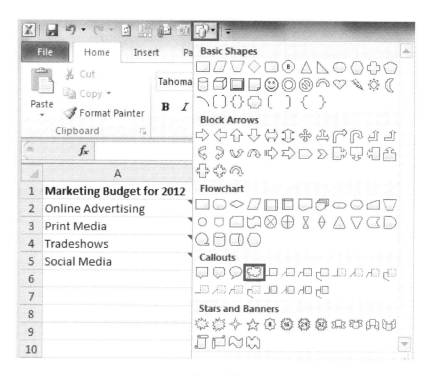

Figure 300

The comment changes from this -

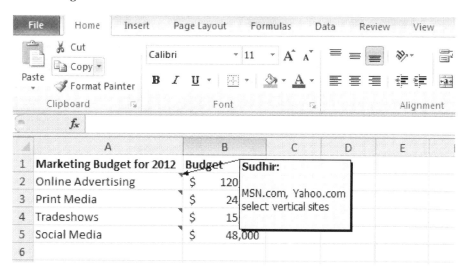

Figure 301

To this -

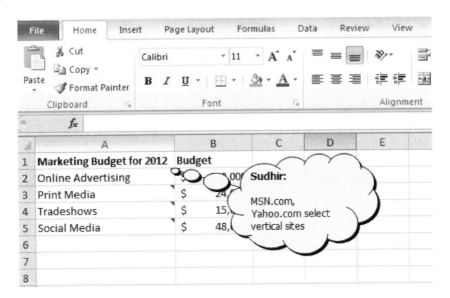

Figure 302

We can have all the comments shaped differently as in the figure below.

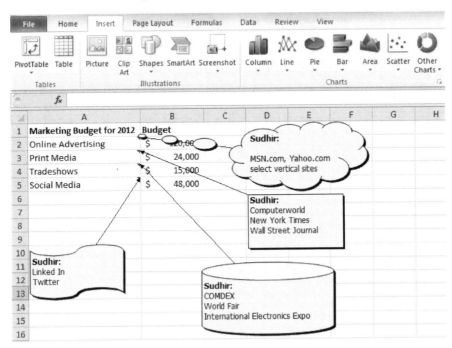

Figure 303

172

87.   Create a Customized Tab – Quick Step for Excel

Here is how to quickly share a workbook.

If you see yourself using the same command many times and you want to cut the number of steps needed, there is an easy way to do it.

Let us say when you are working on a project you have to send the spreadsheet to team members. One of the easiest ways is to send the current file as an attachment.

The steps are as follows:

File, Save & Send, Send Using E-mail, Send as Attachment

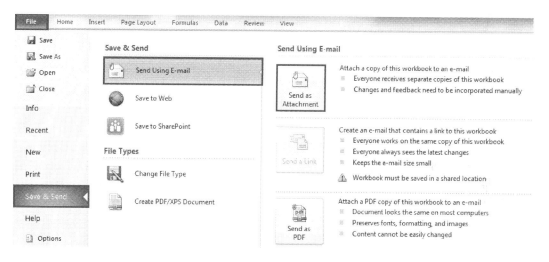

Figure 304

While this is very useful, it can be cumbersome to click four times to do something, if you have to do it repeatedly. In other instances it can take up to seven clicks to get to something you are going to be using very often, depending on your need such as a specific chart of a particularly specific function.

Fortunately for us, the team at Excel has thought about it. Here is where the backstage view comes in handy. Let us add a one-click "Send as Attachment" for Excel.

Step 1: Click File, Options

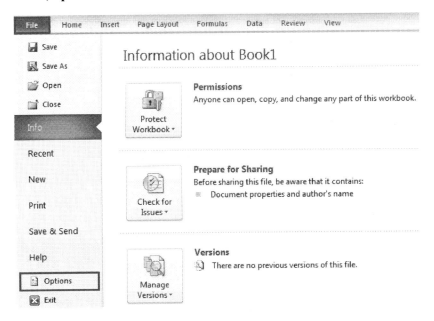

Figure 305

Step 2: Select **Quick Access Toolbar** and click on drop down arrow under **Popular Commands**.

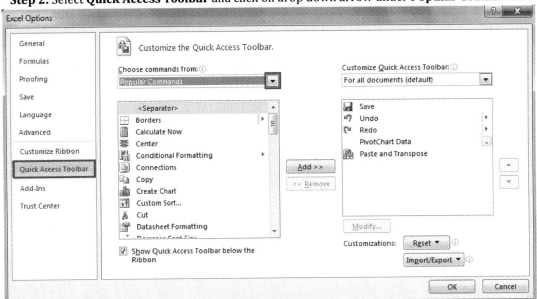

Figure 306

Step 3: Select **All Commands**

Figure 307

Step 4: Select **E-mail and Add**. You can also choose other commands like **E-mail as PDF or E-mail as XPS Attachment.**

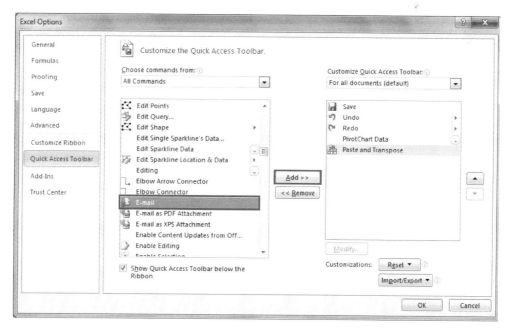

Figure 308

Step 5: Select **OK**. Notice that Quick Access Toolbar is selected on the left. The new icon will be added to the Quick Access Toolbar.

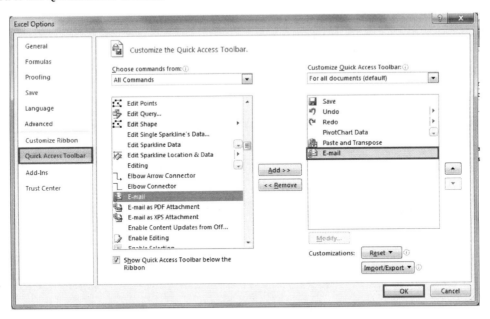

Figure 309

Step 6: The icon to e-mail the sheet as an attachment has been added to the Quick Access Toolbar and can be used to e-mail the workbook with a single click.

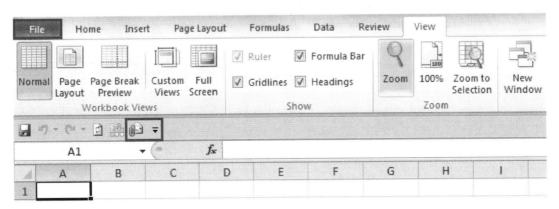

Figure 310

Note: By default all customizations apply to all documents. If you want to apply to a specific workbook, select that from the dropdown, as shown below.

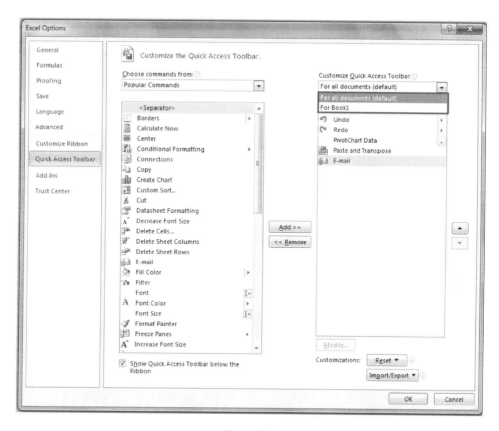

Figure 311

88. Watch Window

While Excel is a fantastic and really easy program to use, Excel spreadsheets have a tendency to get notoriously complex in no time before a user realizes it. As you do complex financial modeling you need to keep track of the final output of a cell. Let us say you are trying to project your company's revenue for the next fiscal year. You may have various spreadsheets with assumptions and calculations for sales channels, marketing expenses, research and development expenses, etc. Like anything in life, you have to optimize your variables for the best result.

If you increase marketing spending by 20% on web channels, you may have to reduce the telesales component. It might have a direct impact on the unit sales you project. You might find yourself scrolling up and down a spreadsheet or switching between spreadsheets to see the results.

Excel has this cool feature called "Watch Window." What it does is opens a small window in which you can monitor the value of a cell. Let me illustrate it with an example and the value of **Watch Window** will be evident.

Let us say you have this spreadsheet with the following model.

Sales = Web + Telesales + Wholesale +Partner-Led sales

Profit = Sales-Cost

	A	B	C	D	E	F	G
1		Web	Telesales	Wholesale	Partner	Total	
2	Sales	$ 3,367,416	$ 400,500	$ 432,000	$ 3,175,500	$ 7,375,416	
3	Cost	$ 2,000,000	$ 320,000	$ 180,000	$ 1,314,000	$ 3,814,000	
4	Profit	$ 1,367,416	$ 80,500	$ 252,000	$ 1,861,500	$ 3,561,416	
5							
6							
7							
8	Web						
9							
10	Month	Traffic	Conversion	Average Per ur	Sales ($)		
11	Jan	735941	2.12%	18	$ 280,835		
12	Feb	694089	2.30%	14	$ 223,497		
13	Mar	234919	2.40%	11	$ 62,019		
14	Apr	161072	2.40%	20	$ 77,315		
15	May	694291	2.40%	15	$ 249,945		
16	Jun	493515	2.50%	17	$ 209,744		
17	Jul	859359	2.70%	19	$ 440,851		
18	Aug	446482	2.70%	18	$ 216,990		
19	Sep	754142	2.70%	14	$ 285,066		
20	Oct	732016	3.00%	16	$ 351,368		
21	Nov	805908	3.00%	20	$ 483,545		
22	Dec	810404	3.00%	20	$ 486,242		
23	Total				$ 3,367,416		
24							
25	Telesales						
26							

Figure 312

Now just like the Web break-out above, you have the sections that break out monthly projection for Telesales, Wholesales, and Partner.

As you change the variables for, say, the number of partners who sell your services, or the number of telesales agents, the Sales and Profit numbers will change. If you are like most users you will end up scrolling up and down to see the impact of the changes that you make "upstream."

Step 1 - To avoid the need, activate the **Watch Window, Formulas, Watch Window**

Figure 313

Step 2 – Click on **Add Watch** and enter the cell whose value you want to watch. In this case, we want to watch Total Sales, in cell F2 from the figure above. Note the exclamation mark in the formula specifies the spreadsheet tab name which for this example I chose as WatchWindow. By default you will see it as Sheet1, Sheet 2 etc.

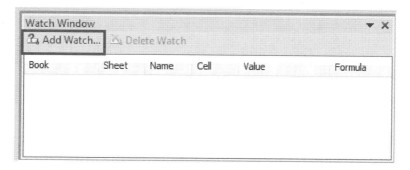

Figure 314

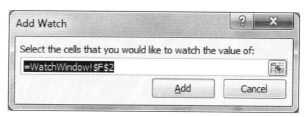

Figure 315

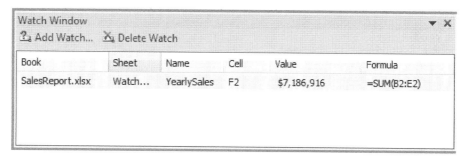

Figure 316

Step 3 – As you can see in the figure below, if you scroll down to row 71 the Watch Window is within view. Now, when you make changes to, say, the number of partners you allocate, you can see the impact of your changes on Total Sales in cell F2 (in figure 312).

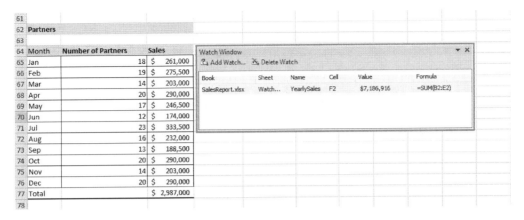

Figure 317

Step 4 – If you change the number of partners to 61 in December the value changes instantly.

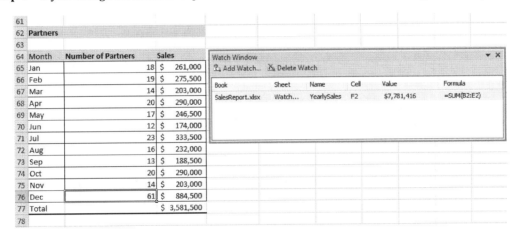

Figure 318

You can add multiple cells to the Watch Window, and also dock the Watch Window just under the ribbon if you want, as shown below.

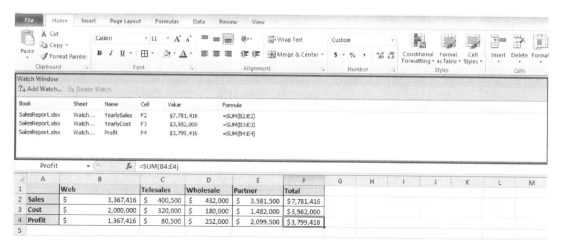

Figure 319

89. Advanced Filter

This is a really powerful feature of Excel. This is very useful if you have a large spreadsheet and you want to filter the output based on a set of criteria to a new location or new spreadsheet.

In this case I open my sales spreadsheet and I want all of the records whose OrderType is Web, and **Region: South,** to be copied to a new sheet. The traditional option is to do a two-step filter, select all, copy and paste into the new sheet. I say, too much work. ☺ Fortunately the Excel team has done some *EXCEL*lent work.

Step 1 – Open the spreadsheet you want to apply advanced filter on – the original sheet.

	A	B	C	D	E	F	G	H	I
1	Month	Year	Category	Salesperson	Region	Sales	Units	Discount	OrderType
2	January	2001	Automotive	Ken	West	$ 7,289	30	18%	Web
3	February	2001	Electronics	Dan	East	$ 7,249	16	15%	Retail
4	March	2001	Automotive	Jan	East	$ 7,212	5	19%	Wholesale
5	April	2001	Apparel	Brian	South	$ 7,172	72	19%	Retail
6	May	2001	Childrens	Andy	North	$ 7,110	58	16%	Retail
7	June	2001	Home	Karen	East	$ 6,996	182	19%	Retail
8	July	2001	Garden	Ryan	West	$ 6,973	150	18%	Web
9	August	2001	Tools	Sachin	East	$ 6,971	188	20%	Retail
10	September	2001	Electronics	Amitabh	East	$ 6,868	185	16%	Retail
11	October	2001	Toys	Kris	North	$ 6,806	156	19%	Web
12	November	2001	Automotive	Dey	West	$ 6,744	186	18%	Wholesale
13	December	2003	Electronics	Taylor	South	$ 6,373	175	14%	Wholesale
14	January	2001	Automtive	Tom	North	$ 6,361	202	19%	Phone
15	February	2005	Apparel	Karen	East	$ 6,227	159	19%	Phone
16	March	2001	Childrens	Ken	West	$ 6,215	190	15%	Phone
17	April	2001	Home	Karen	East	$ 6,167	176	8%	Web
18	May	2002	Garden	Taylor	South	$ 6,149	140	19%	Retail
19	June	2001	Tools	Brian	South	$ 6,111	188	14%	Retail

Figure 320

Step 2 – Select all of the data and go to **Data, Advanced Filter**

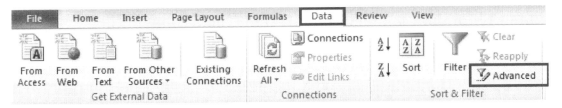

Figure 321

Step 3 – Enter the **List range, Criteria** and **Output range**

Figure 322

Go to a location in the spreadsheet and enter the criteria. One important thing to note is to have the title of the columns for the criteria definition match the one in the spreadsheet. The formula will fetch all data from your criteria set.

Figure 323

Since I selected the file as Copy to another location I chose Cell Q1:Y1

The output appears as follows. Notice that it has all of the column headings, but contains only data that is both OrderType:Web and Region: South.

Q	R	S	T	U	V	W	X	Y
Month	Year	Category	Salesperson	Region	Sales	Units	Discount	OrderType
July	2001	Electronics	Kory	South	$ 6,080	189	19%	Web
Novembe	2002	Childrens	Kory	South	$ 5,357	146	15%	Web
May	2004	Garden	Sanjay	South	$ 1,256	39	3%	Web
July	2004	Electronics	Gabriel	South	$ 6,080	189	19%	Web

Figure 324

This is really powerful if, say, you have a spreadsheet with 2000 rows and 20 columns, and each stakeholder only cares about their specific set of filtered records.

90.   Sensitivity Analysis

Let us say you are projecting the number of conversions from an e-mail campaign. I reused the example from an earlier tip with the formula highlighted for cell B6.

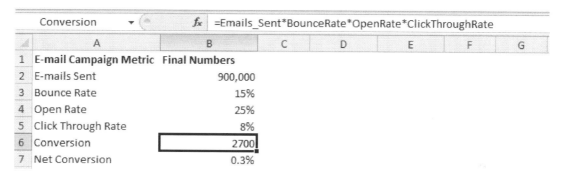

Figure 325

There are two or three key variables based on the e-mail list purchased, subject line, creative, offer, etc.

- Emails Sent
- Open Rate
- Click-Through Rate

You will want to optimize the results for your campaigns. One might want to model a scenario based on how the conversion changes if our current open rate of 25% varies between 16% to 30%? Also, how does it change if the e-mail purchased is changed from 900,000 to 1,250,000?

One way is to manually enter the formulas. But creating the grid is a nightmare unless you used advanced functions. The other way is Data Tables.

Data Tables allow you to see the sensitivity of a combination or combinations of variables. Here are the steps to generate the data table.

Step 1 - To set up a one-way data table, list the input values in a column. In this case we list the open rate from 16% to 30% in cells B11:B25.

In cells C10, D10 enter the formula for the Emails Opened and Conversion as follows.

Emails Opened = Emails_Sent*BounceRate*OpenRate
Conversion = =Emails_Sent*BounceRate*OpenRate*ClickThroughRate

Label the columns in Cell C9 and D9. The setup is very important.

Step 2 – Select cells B10 to D25

	A	B	C	D
1	E-mail Campaign Metric	Final Numbers		
2	E-mails Sent	900,000		
3	Bounce Rate	15%		
4	Open Rate	25%		
5	Click Through Rate	8%		
6	Conversion	2700		
7	Net Conversion	0.3%		
8				
9			Emails Opened	Conversion
10			33750	2700
11		16%		
12		17%		
13		18%		
14		19%		
15		20%		
16		21%		
17		22%		
18		23%		
19		24%		
20		25%		
21		26%		
22		27%		
23		28%		
24		29%		
25		30%		

Figure 326

and go to **Data, What If Analysis, Data Table**

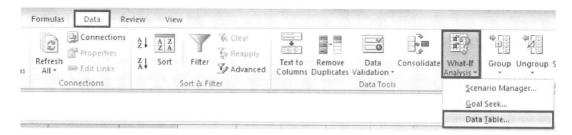

Figure 327

Step 3 – Select cell B4 in the column input to tell Excel that this is the cell that will be changing – our 25% Open Rate.

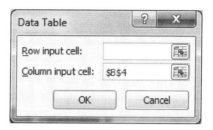

Figure 328

Excel will dynamically replace the cell value with the column on the left to create a data table.

	A	B	C	D	E
1	E-mail Campaign Metric	Final Numbers			
2	E-mails Sent	900,000			
3	Bounce Rate	15%			
4	Open Rate	25%			
5	Click Through Rate	8%			
6	Conversion	2700			
7	Net Conversion	0.3%			
8					
9			Emails Opened	Conversion	
10			33750	2700	
11		16%	21600	1728	
12		17%	22950	1836	
13		18%	24300	1944	
14		19%	25650	2052	
15		20%	27000	2160	
16		21%	28350	2268	
17		22%	29700	2376	
18		23%	31050	2484	
19		24%	32400	2592	
20		25%	33750	2700	
21		26%	35100	2808	
22		27%	36450	2916	
23		28%	37800	3024	
24		29%	39150	3132	
25		30%	40500	3240	

Figure 329

To create a two-way data table that shows the number of e-mails and open rate, set the table with the rows B9-D9 filled with the number of e-mails sent. The important thing to note is that the formula be entered in the corner cell B9 in this case.

Again go to **Data, What-If Analysis, Data Table**

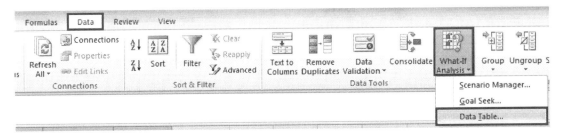

Figure 330

Select the Row and Input cells.

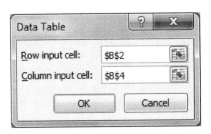

Figure 331

The output is as follows. Now you can see what combination of open rate and e-mails will give you the optimum results you need for your campaign.

B10	fx	=Emails_Sent*BounceRate*OpenRate* ClickThroughRate										
	B	C	D	E	F	G	H	I	J	K	L	M
10	2700	750,000	800,000	850,000	900,000	950,000	1,000,000	1,050,000	1,100,000	1,150,000	1,200,000	1,250,000
11	16%	1440	1536	1632	1728	1824	1920	2016	2112	2208	2304	2400
12	17%	1530	1632	1734	1836	1938	2040	2142	2244	2346	2448	2550
13	18%	1620	1728	1836	1944	2052	2160	2268	2376	2484	2592	2700
14	19%	1710	1824	1938	2052	2166	2280	2394	2508	2622	2736	2850
15	20%	1800	1920	2040	2160	2280	2400	2520	2640	2760	2880	3000
16	21%	1890	2016	2142	2268	2394	2520	2646	2772	2898	3024	3150
17	22%	1980	2112	2244	2376	2508	2640	2772	2904	3036	3168	3300
18	23%	2070	2208	2346	2484	2622	2760	2898	3036	3174	3312	3450
19	24%	2160	2304	2448	2592	2736	2880	3024	3168	3312	3456	3600
20	25%	2250	2400	2550	2700	2850	3000	3150	3300	3450	3600	3750
21	26%	2340	2496	2652	2808	2964	3120	3276	3432	3588	3744	3900
22	27%	2430	2592	2754	2916	3078	3240	3402	3564	3726	3888	4050
23	28%	2520	2688	2856	3024	3192	3360	3528	3696	3864	4032	4200
24	29%	2610	2784	2958	3132	3306	3480	3654	3828	4002	4176	4350
25	30%	2700	2880	3060	3240	3420	3600	3780	3960	4140	4320	4500

Figure 332

91. What-If Analysis – Goal Seek

What if (no pun intended) you already have an end goal in mind. For example, given the variables, you wonder what the input should be to reach a certain goal? In some cases mental math is sufficient. But occasionally you will need a scenario where you want the goal calculated more precisely.

Let us say you want to know, if you have 786,786 e-mail addresses and the bounce rate is 7.86%, what should the click-through rate be to get 2,912 conversions? This assumes the open rate is 25%. Note the numbers in the example below have been deliberately chosen to make mental math harder, but if you are god's gift to calculation, please go ahead and bypass this tip. The rest of us can use the Goal Seek command. ☺

Set up the formula as follows.

	Conversion	▼	f_x	=Emails_Sent*BounceRate*OpenRate* ClickThroughRate		
	A	B	C	D	E	F
2	E-mails Sent	786,786				
3	Bounce Rate	7.86%				
4	Open Rate	25%				
5	Click Through Rate	8%				
6	Conversion	1237				
7	Net Conversion	0.2%				
8						

Figure 333

Now if you want 2,912 conversions then roughly we can say that your click-through rate should be around 19%, but to get the exact number. follow these steps.

Step 1 – Go to **Data, What-If Analysis, Goal Seek**

Figure 334

Step 2

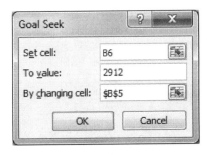

Figure 335

In Step 2, we want to make our conversion rate (B6) hit our goal of 2,912 by changing our click-through rate. Here is the output. You need a click-through rate of 18.84% or higher to get your conversion goal.

	A	B
1	**E-mail Campaign Metric**	**Final Numbers**
2	E-mails Sent	786,786
3	Bounce Rate	7.86%
4	Open Rate	25%
5	Click Through Rate	18.84%
6	Conversion	2912
7	Net Conversion	0.4%

Figure 336

92. What-If Analysis – Scenario Manager

We will continue the same example, but in this case you want to list out the scenario in a summary. How does the conversion change if we change the number of e-mails sent to 1,250,000, but the open rate drops to 22% and the click-through goes to 17%. Let us name this scenario – **Bulk e-mail model**.

Another scenario is 800,000 e-mails with 27% open rate and 22% click-through rate. Let us call this scenario **Statistical model,** that the company's data analytics team has put in place.

	Conversion	▼	⊙	f_x	=Emails_Sent*BounceRate*OpenRate* ClickThroughRate		

▲	A	B	C	D	E	F
1	**E-mail Campaign Metric**	**Final Numbers**				
2	E-mails Sent	900,000				
3	Bounce Rate	10%				
4	Open Rate	25%				
5	Click Through Rate	18.84%				
6	Conversion	4238				
7	Net Conversion	0.5%				
8						

Figure 337

Step 1 – Go to **Data, What-If Analysis, Scenario Manager**

Figure 338

Step 2 – Enter the Value of the scenarios and name them.

Figure 339

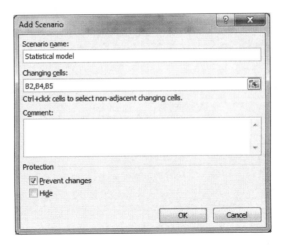

Figure 340

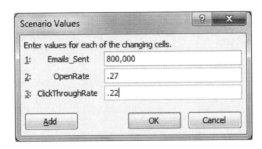

Figure 341

Figure 342

Here is what the output looks like. You can quickly compare the models at a glance.

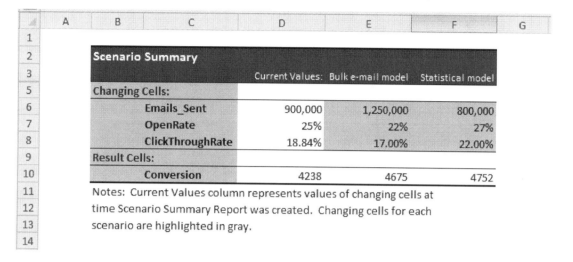

Figure 343

93. vlookup, hlookup

Even though I have a section on functions in the appendix, these deserve special mention. Vlookup and Hlookup stand for Vertical lookup and Horizontal lookup and are very useful to look up data. The more you use them the more you can see how valuable they are.

Let us say you have the top cities in the United States with its state.

	A	B	C
1	City	State	Abbreviation
2	New York	New York	
3	Los Angeles	California	
4	Chicago	Illinois	
5	Houston	Texas	
6	Philadelphia	Pennsylvania	
7	Phoenix	Arizona	
8	San Diego	California	
9	San Antonio	Texas	
10	Dallas	Texas	
11	Detroit	Michigan	
12	San Jose	California	
13	Indianapolis	Indiana	
14	Jacksonville	Florida	
15	San Francisco	California	
16	Columbus	Ohio	
17	Austin	Texas	
18	Memphis	Tennessee	
19	Baltimore	Maryland	
20	Milwaukee	Wisconsin	
21	Fort Worth	Texas	

Figure 344

And let us say you have the standard abbreviations in another table sorted in the ascending order of the state name (shown below in the truncated form)

Figure 345

You want the two-letter state abbreviation next to your cities. To fill in the value of the abbreviation, use the Vlookup function. Move the cursor to cell C2 and enter the following formula: =vlookup and hit CTRL A.

The Vlookup wizard pops up.

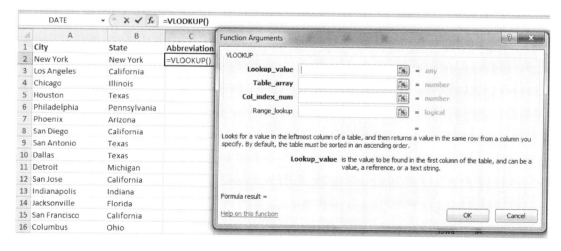

Figure 346

Enter the following values:

In the Lookup_ value enter =B2,

In Table-array enter $J$2:$K$51

In Col_index_num, enter 2, which means enter the value in the second column. And click OK

Range is optional and we can ignore it.

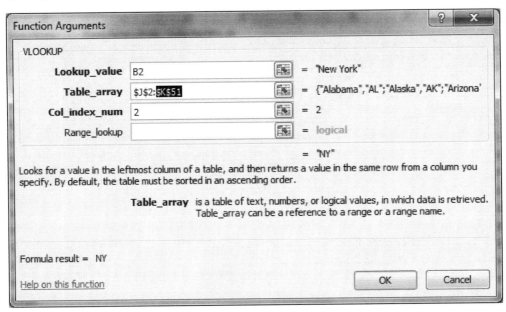

Figure 347

Double click to fill the values all the way to the last city and the state abbreviations are filled automatically as Excel looks up the value and then populates the correct abbreviation based on the state match.

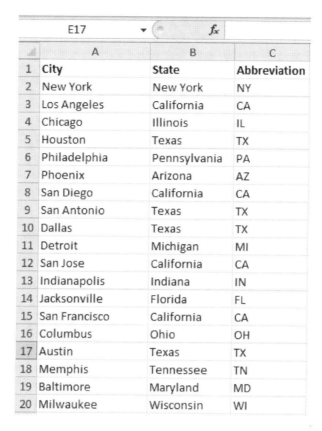

	A	B	C
1	**City**	**State**	**Abbreviation**
2	New York	New York	NY
3	Los Angeles	California	CA
4	Chicago	Illinois	IL
5	Houston	Texas	TX
6	Philadelphia	Pennsylvania	PA
7	Phoenix	Arizona	AZ
8	San Diego	California	CA
9	San Antonio	Texas	TX
10	Dallas	Texas	TX
11	Detroit	Michigan	MI
12	San Jose	California	CA
13	Indianapolis	Indiana	IN
14	Jacksonville	Florida	FL
15	San Francisco	California	CA
16	Columbus	Ohio	OH
17	Austin	Texas	TX
18	Memphis	Tennessee	TN
19	Baltimore	Maryland	MD
20	Milwaukee	Wisconsin	WI

Figure 348

Hlookup is similar, except it looks at values horizontally.

94.   Text to Columns

If you get a list of addresses or names and you want to separate, say, the first name from the last name, to create a mailing to use with Outlook for mail merge purposes, here are the steps.

We begin with the list of names as shown below:

Figure 349

Step 1: Go to **Data, Text to Columns**

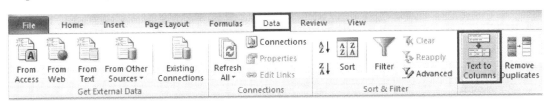

Figure 350

Step 2: Walk through the wizard.

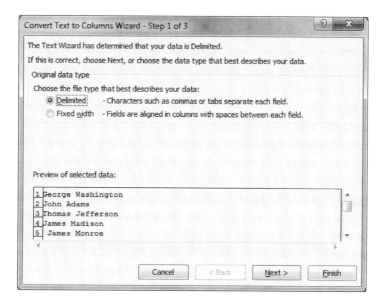

Figure 351

In the second step of the wizard, check **Other** and hit Enter to tell Excel to treat each space as the beginning of a new column, and click **Next.**

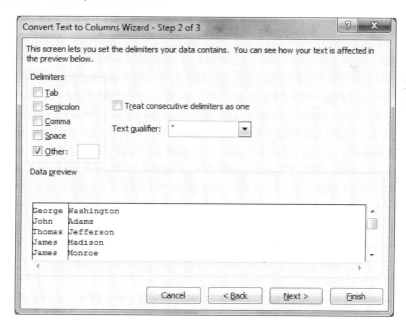

Figure 352

In step 3 of the wizard you can leave the column data as General, and Finish.

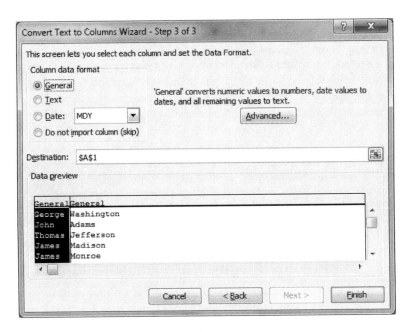

Figure 353

The data has been split into two columns.

	A	B
1	George	Washington
2	John	Adams
3	Thomas	Jefferson
4	James	Madison
5	James	Monroe
6	John	Tyler
7	James	Polk
8	Zachary	Taylor
9	Millard	Fillmore
10	Franklin	Pierce
11	James	Buchanan
12	Abraham	Lincoln
13	Andrew	Johnson
14	Ulysses	Grant
15	Rutherford	Hayes
16	James	Garfield
17	Bill	Clinton
18	Grover	Cleveland
19	Benjamin	Harrison

Figure 354

95. Views

In most large companies Excel workbooks are the default collaborative tool with inputs from various departments, regions (countries and districts in larger geographies), product groups, sales channels, etc. It is expected for any multi-billion dollar company to have this level of rigor in its DNA.

Whenever a final document or close-to-final document is shared, everyone who is required to sign off on the document quickly wants to dive into their areas and regions. Some of these workbooks can be really big. When I mean big, trust me, they are truly works of data-crunching art.

One way to make the workbooks more useful and appealing to the various stakeholders is to use Views.

I am using a simplistic example but you will get the idea. Here is a sample sales-planning tool.

	A	B	C	D	E	F
	North			South		
2	City	Sales		City	Sales	
3	Minneapolis	$ 224,414.00		Dallas	$ 214,117.00	
4	Detroit	$ 104,361.00		Lubbock	$ 94,387.00	
5	Chicago	$ 154,933.00		Houston	$ 197,824.00	
6	Total	$ 483,708.00		Baton Rouge	$ 147,554.00	
7				Total	$ 653,882.00	
8						
9						
10	East			West		
11	City	Sales		City	Sales	
12	New York	$ 110,659.00		Los Angeles	$ 121,350.00	
13	Boston	$ 112,397.00		Seattle	$ 73,943.00	
14	Baltimore	$ 242,031.00		Portland	$ 215,726.00	
15	Miami	$ 146,360.00		SanFrancisco	$ 101,701.00	
16	Atlanta	$ 212,046.00		San Diego	$ 148,889.00	
17	Orlando	$ 235,719.70		Total	$ 661,609.00	
18	Total	$ 1,059,212.70				
19						
20						

Figure 355

Now imagine if the person in the East region only wants to see his view. To achieve this, go to **View**, and create a **Custom View** called "East."

Figure 356

You will see a pop-up window.

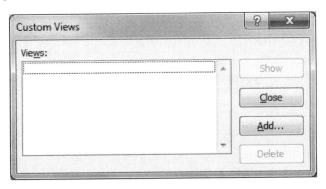

Figure 357

For the East view we will hide all the extraneous rows and columns, name the view, and click OK.

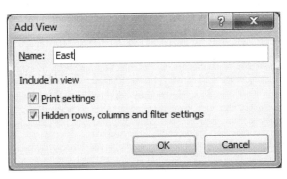

Figure 358

Now when you select Custom Views you can select and zoom into a specific view.

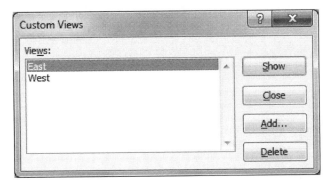

Figure 359

This is a very simple example, but Custom Views can really be very useful if you want to save custom settings and headers. Here is what the output looks like for us.

	A	B	C
10		East	
11	City	Sales	
12	New York	$ 110,659.00	
13	Boston	$ 112,397.00	
14	Baltimore	$ 242,031.00	
15	Miami	$ 146,360.00	
16	Atlanta	$ 212,046.00	
17	Orlando	$ 235,719.70	
18	Total	$ 1,059,212.70	
19			

Figure 360

96. Custom Ordering of the PivotTable

In a PivotTable you will have values sorted as ascending by default. You normally can change it to descending as the other option. For example in our sales report PivotTable, the regions are sorted alphabetically: East, North, South, and West.

	A	B	C
1			
2	OrderType	(All) ▼	
3	Year	(All) ▼	
4			
5		Values	
6	Region ▼	Sum of Sales	Sum of Units
7	East	$88,194	2054
8	North	$57,647	1400
9	South	$91,046	2314
10	West	$76,610	1863
11	Grand Total	$313,497	7631

Figure 361

It works in most cases. Now what if we had fifty cities with Albuquerque and Austin at the top and New York in the middle and Washington DC at the bottom. If you really wanted to see how the sales of your products were in the top cities you would probably like New York and Washington DC to be near the top of any Pivot. The trick is to simply type the city's name at the cell where you want it to be, and the PivotTable will remember your selection.

In my example, if I want the PivotTable to always list West at the top, all I do is move the active cell to A7 and type "West". Now my PivotTable always shows West as the first row, as shown in the two examples below.

▲	A	B	C	
1				
2	OrderType	(All) ▼		
3	Year	(All) ▼		
4				
5		**Values**		
6	**Region** ▼	**Sum of Sales**	**Sum of Units**	
7	West	$76,610	1863	
8	East	$88,194	2054	
9	North	$57,647	1400	
10	South	$91,046	2314	
11	**Grand Total**	**$313,497**	**7631**	

Figure 362

Another example of the same -

▲	A	B	C	D	E
1					
2	OrderType	(All) ▼			
3	Year	(All) ▼			
4					
5			**Values**		
6	**Region** ▼	**Category** ↲	**Sum of Sales**	**Sum of Units**	
7	⊟**West**	Automotive	$20,777	402	
8		Childrens	$18,198	511	
9		Toys	$16,469	401	
10		Apparel	$11,217	340	
11		Garden	$6,973	150	
12		Tools	$2,976	59	
13	**West Total**		**$76,610**	**1863**	
14	⊟**East**	Electronics	$25,257	520	
15		Home	$25,094	713	
16		Automotive	$12,656	156	
17		Apparel	$12,454	318	
18		Tools	$6,971	188	
19		Garden	$5,762	159	
20	**East Total**		**$88,194**	**2054**	

Figure 363

97.   Creating a Frequency Distribution based on a PivotTable

Sometimes it is more efficient to understand how your data is sorted by bands. So if you have sales transactions you want to know what is your "sweet spot" is, or where is the most likely average deal going to be. You can get the same via a histogram, but it has to change every time you change your bands.

To illustrate this I will analyze the "Sales" by "Sales person" data, to see how sales are distributed in ranges of $500 bands, and how many salespersons are in the $0-$500, $500-$1,000 and so on.

Step 1: The first thing: to create a frequency distribution, have the raw values in the "Row" area of the PivotTable and not in the "Values" area.

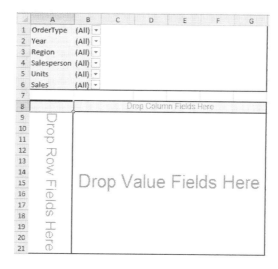

Figure 364

Next drop the Sales in the Row area and right-click on any cell, say A9, and select **Group**

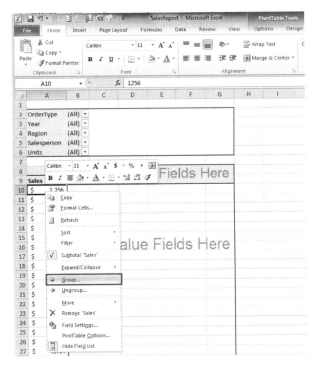

Figure 365

Step 2: Enter the frequency bands. Excel will automatically fill the lowest value as the starting and maximum value as the highest. I changed it to begin at $0 and end at $8,000 and band increments at $500.

Figure 366

Now you have the frequency bands. Note there is nothing in the 0-500 and 500-1000 bands, as there is no value in the PivotTable that corresponds to it. So Excel automatically removes it.

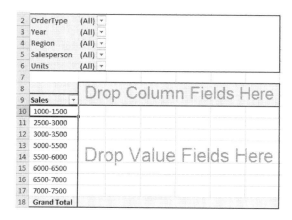

Figure 367

Step 3: Drag the Sales to the **Value** area and you can see the frequency distribution.

	A	B	C
1			
2	OrderType	(All) ▾	
3	Year	(All) ▾	
4	Region	(All) ▾	
5	Salesperson	(All) ▾	
6	Units	(All) ▾	
7			
8	**Count of Sales**		
9	**Sales** ▾	**Total**	
10	1000-1500	1	
11	2500-3000	1	
12	3000-3500	1	
13	5000-5500	9	
14	5500-6000	13	
15	6000-6500	16	
16	6500-7000	7	
17	7000-7500	5	
18	**Grand Total**	53	
19			

Figure 368

98.   Hide the Cell content without hiding the Column.

Now this one is one of the Power Tips you learn after years of paying your dues in Excel. Every now and then you have a need to hide the values of a cell, but not the column. But for exactness of the calculation you want to let the value remain in there, as all of the aggregations are dependent on the same.

Say you have the sales projections for various cities in the East region, and you have incorporated Puerto Rico and the Bahamas as you are expanding in these new territories. But sales there will be negligible, hence you may want to hide those values to display the data more cleanly.

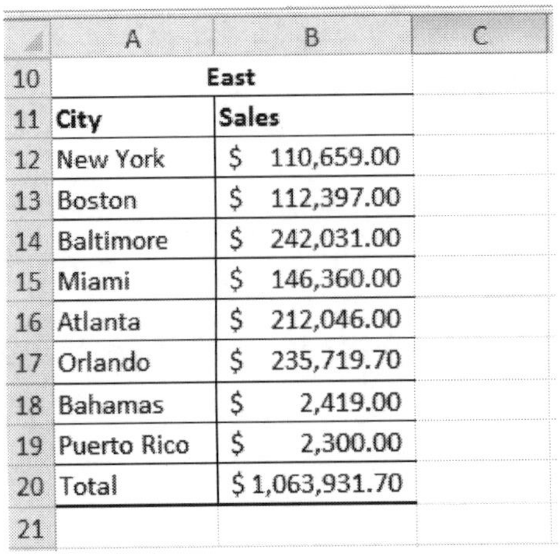

	A	B	C
10		East	
11	City	Sales	
12	New York	$ 110,659.00	
13	Boston	$ 112,397.00	
14	Baltimore	$ 242,031.00	
15	Miami	$ 146,360.00	
16	Atlanta	$ 212,046.00	
17	Orlando	$ 235,719.70	
18	Bahamas	$ 2,419.00	
19	Puerto Rico	$ 2,300.00	
20	Total	$ 1,063,931.70	
21			

Figure 369

If you want to hide the value for Bahamas and Puerto Rico, just select the cells and click Format, Custom, and Enter three semi-colons (;;;) and click OK.

The cell contents won't be visible but can be used in formulas and are still visible in the formula bar as shown below.

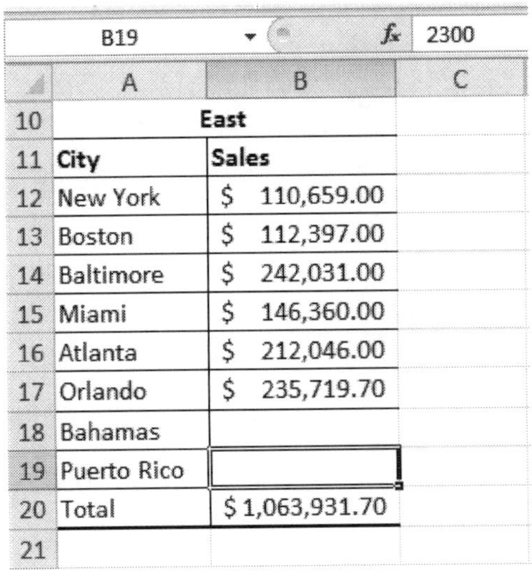

B19	▾	f_x	2300

	A	B	C
10		East	
11	City	Sales	
12	New York	$ 110,659.00	
13	Boston	$ 112,397.00	
14	Baltimore	$ 242,031.00	
15	Miami	$ 146,360.00	
16	Atlanta	$ 212,046.00	
17	Orlando	$ 235,719.70	
18	Bahamas		
19	Puerto Rico		
20	Total	$ 1,063,931.70	
21			

Figure 370

99. Excel Camera Tool

I thought a lot about which should be the last tip in the book, and zeroed in on the Camera tool within Excel. This is one of those little-known tools which, when used correctly, can significantly impact your productivity and also wow your colleagues and friends alike.

Here is the case where this tip is most useful. Let us say you have a set of charts in a table and the chart change based on a value. If we want to see how the charts change based on a certain value, it would be good to see real-time change in the charts where we are making the change. The closest analogy is Picture-in Picture mode in televisions. Let us dive straight into the tool.

Here is a spreadsheet which has a sales projection for a book. We can chart the break-even point.

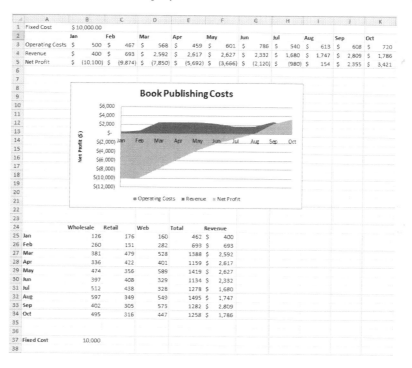

Figure 371

Now when I change the fixed costs, or the sales by channel, my chart changes. Imagine this spreadsheet to be so big that the chart is located too far away to fit into a single screen. Hence with every change you have to scroll up or down to see the breakeven point. With the camera tool you can see a small slice of the Excel sheet right next to where you are making the change. Here are the steps.

Step 1- Go **to File, Options, Quick Access Tool Bar**. Select All commands, Locate the **Camera Tool** and Click **Add, OK** as shown in the figure.

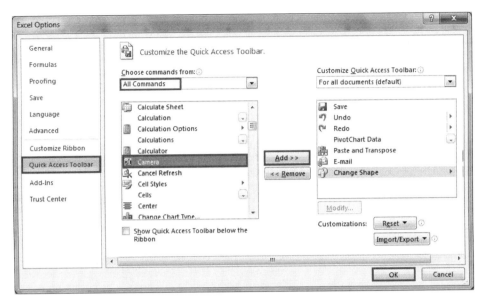

Figure 372

Once you exit the screen your Quick Access Toolbar should look like this with a Camera icon.

Figure 373

Step 2 - Select the cells next to the chart – in this example cell range B7-H22, and click on the **Camera tool icon**.

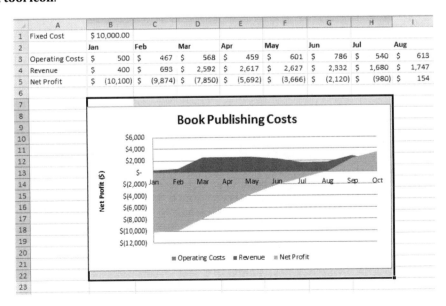

Figure 374

Step 3- Click in the Excel sheet where you want to place the snap shot, in this case cell D37, and resize the screenshot to your needs to get a living Microchart.

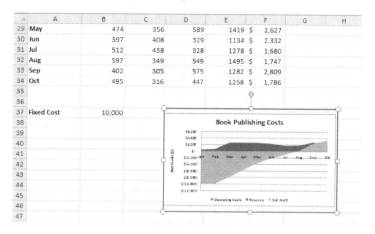

Figure 375

Now as I change the fixed cost to, say, $7,500 or $11,000, I can see the chart updating dynamically.

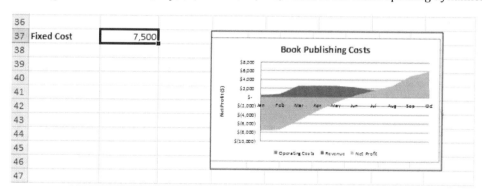

Figure 376

There you have it – 99 Priceless Tips on Excel. And if you have been persistent enough to come to Tip 99, your Excel skill level should be significantly improved. Not only this, but also you should be one of the go-to people in your workplace for Excel.

Please review and refer to these tips many times, until they become second nature. The best way to learn is to teach someone else. And continue your learning using some of the blogs, books and websites mentioned in the appendix.

Extras

Excel Functions

Here are some useful Excel functions you can use in your day-to-day work. I have found many of them very useful and it saves me the trouble of looking them up if I have them handy.

Functions	Description	Example
SUMIF	Returns the sum value from a specified range that meets a criteria	If a range of cells A1:A4 contained values Sudhir,2,9,2 then SUMIF(A1:A4,2) will return 4 as it sums cells with value 2 in it.
COUNTIF	Returns the count from a specified range that meets a criteria	If a range of cells A1:A4 contained values Sudhir, 2, 9, 2 then SUMIF(A1:A4,2) will return 2 as it counts cells with value 2 in it.
TRIM	Removes spaces from start and end of text string. It removes all except single spaces between words	
REPT	Repetitively print a character in a cell	=REPT("*",15) will print an asterisk 15 times in a cell
CONVERT	Converts from imperial to metric units or vice versa	=CONVERT(100,"mi","km") will convert 100 miles to 160.934 km
WORKDAY	Calculates the workday after certain number of days	=WORKDAY (TODAY(),45) will return the date of the workday after 45 days. It automatically excludes weekends.
NOW()	Returns the current time	
TODAY()	Returns the current date	
EXACT	Compares two cells	=EXACT(A2,A3) returns TRUE if the cells are identical and FALSE if they are different
COUNTA	Returns the number of non-empty cells in a range	
COUNTBLANK	Returns the number of blank cells in a range	
INDEX	INDEX returns the cell value based on the Row and Column number	If you have months from A1:A12 INDEX(A1:A12,4) will return APRIL, the fourth month.
SEARCH	Searches a text within a text and tells the position of the letter	=SEARCH("D", Cell reference) where the cell contains "Sudhir" will return 3
© www.vyanjan.com		

Cheat Sheets

Microsoft Excel®2010

Task	Quick Key
New e-mail message	CTRL+N
New file	Ctrl + N
Open file	Ctrl + O
Save file	Ctrl + S
Move between open workbooks	Ctrl + F6
Close file	Ctrl + F4
Save as	F12
Display the print menu	Ctrl + P
Select whole spreadsheet	Ctrl + A
Select column	Ctrl + Space
Select row	Shift + Space
Undo last action	Ctrl + Z
Redo last action	Ctrl + Y
Start a formula	Equals Sign (e.g. =SUM(A1+A2)
Close selected workbook	CTRL+W
Insert Hyperlink	CTRL+K
Apply the percentage format	Ctrl + Shift+%
Apply the currency format	Ctrl + Shift+$
Hide rows	Ctrl + 9
Hide columns	Ctrl+0
Apply the outline border	Ctrl + Shift+&
Enter time	Ctrl + :
Display all formulas	Ctrl + ~
© www.vyanjan.com	

Appendix

The Windows Graphical User Interface

The diagram below shows the elements and standard terminology of the Windows Graphical User Interface.

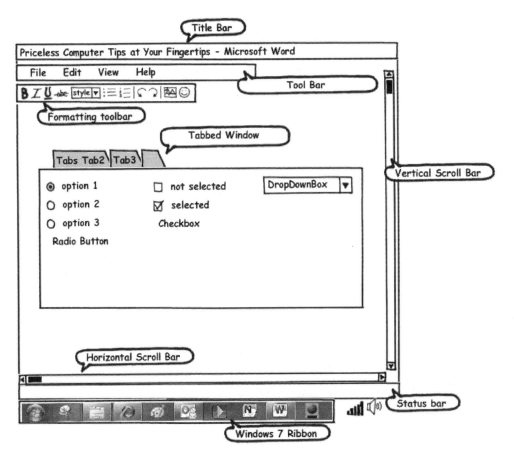

Figure 377

The Excel Graphical User Interface

The diagram below shows the elements and standard terminology of the Excel Graphical User Interface.

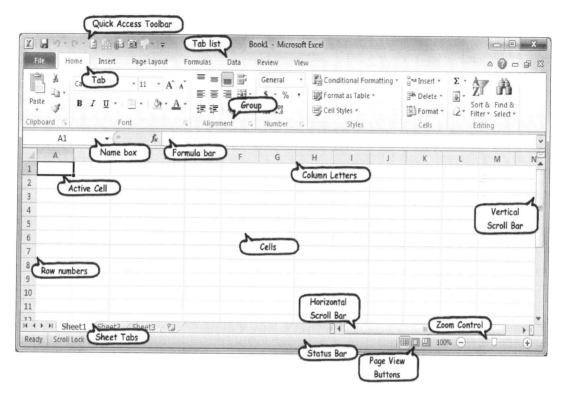

Figure 378

What is a "Right Click" on a mouse?

Most Windows applications use the mouse's "Right Click" to activate very helpful, commonly used sub-menus or commands. The diagram below indicates the Right Click on a mouse.

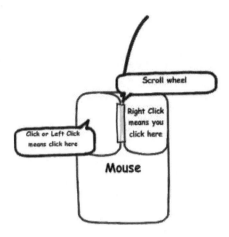

Figure 379

Useful Sites & Books

These links are provided for your convenience. The author has no responsibility for the content of the linked website(s) and books.

Microsoft Office Site http://office.microsoft.com/en-us/
Lots of free templates, background designs, and tips on using the various Microsoft Office products.

Microsoft Most Valuable Professional (MVP) Blog sites - http://www.mvps.org/links.html
A treasury of sites and links to possibly the most dedicated and selfless army of experts on various Microsoft products serving the community. Definitely my favorite site.

Microsoft Excel 2010: Data Analysis and Business Modeling by Wayne L. Winston– I was fortunate enough to attend one of Professor Winston's classes which helped me take Advanced Excel Analysis to a whole new level. If you cannot attend one of his classes, get this book.

John Walkenbach's site – I have learned a lot from John Walkenbach's books over the past decade or so: http://spreadsheetpage.com/index.php/blog/

Bill Jelen's Mr. Excel site
Your definitive guide to advanced Excel resources, help and how-to tips. www.mrexcel.com

Pointy-Haired Geek http://www.chandoo.org/
This gem of a site covers a broad range of Excel tips from a wide variety of topics such as charts, templates, and shortcuts. A must-read for new users.

Abela, Andrew V. **Advanced Presentations by Design: Creating Communication That Drives Action**. San Francisco, CA: Pfeiffer, 2008.

Book Ordering

If you would like to order more copies of this book, please visit www.vyanjan.com or send an e-mail to book@vyanjan.com

Made in the USA
San Bernardino, CA
30 November 2017